Creating a million change makers

Introduction

I love my job. Every day, I get to help and support people dealing with some of the most difficult challenges they'll ever face, both professionally and personally.

The volume of change that individuals experience in their personal lives continues to accelerate at an amazing pace...and from all angles. Cultural and societal change, environmental change, economic and political change, technology change as well as the health, physical, emotional and developmental changes life brings automatically.

Change can be complex, critical, challenging, confusing and confounding AND it can be exciting, exhilarating, energising and fun! However it impacts us, it is reassuring to know that most of us have a choice when it comes to how we respond. I say most of us because there are many around us without the capacity or the capability to deal with change. For individuals in their personal lives, the sense of overwhelm is almost at epidemic levels and within organisations, no sooner has one change been understood another is queuing up, waiting to be implemented.

Many of the Change Makers in this book started their professional careers when change management was seen as the last thing on the To Do List as organisations implemented major change, almost an after-thought. Increasingly, it became obvious that the negative impacts of change could be significantly reduced and the positive opportunities amplified if change management was elevated to the top of the list.

When we set our mission to "Create a million Change Makers" it was because we recognised that more and more people need other people to help them make sense of it all, see the opportunities and just walk alongside them as they take the next step. Change Wisdom is your virtual guide through many dimensions of change, both corporate and personal, and will provide you with a volume of valuable insights. The aim of the book is simple, to help and support YOU. Please contact us and let us know how you are getting on; we'd love to share your experiences to help others and are always here if we can help you further.

Best wishes,

Simon Phillips
Founder of The Change Maker Group
simon@thechangemakergroup.com

community@thechangemakergroup.com

Contents

NOTES FROM THE CURATOR

on

Change Wisdom
Insights from successful Change Makers to guide your future

When the idea of this book was mooted we asked some of our Change Makers to write about a subject that they feel passionate about that impacts on change initiatives. Although change is more ubiquitous and challenging today we have better knowledge of how we react (and often why we don't react) to change. In general leaders are more willing to meet it head on. But still it seems as tricky as ever.

These chapters are 'individual shots' of wisdom on change, taken from different viewpoints , from many years of experience each Change Maker has in working in this field. Each chapter stands on its own as a thought piece so you can dip in and out depending on what you feel will address your need. We separate them into 3 change themes:

- Strategic Change
- Change Management
- How we as Individuals deal with change.

Although it is not always clear where Strategic Change ends and Change Management starts it is a useful indicator of how root and branch the change will be. And always we, as individuals who are involved with change, can learn how better to survive in this dynamic world!

When I came to read them all together, however, it was clear that there are 2 golden threads that run through all 14 chapters.

1. How Change is approached will determine your success

The good news is you don't have to be a slave to change as Malcolm Follos points out in *Vision Missions and All That Jazz*. He shows how important it is to identify what you want your destination to be, only then should you chart your change journey. This hypothesis is picked up by Richard Flewitt in *Establish Solid Foundations for Positive Culture and Change* as he illustrates with several case studies that only when you understand your brand can you have a purposeful relationship with change.

community@thechangemakergroup.com

Several authors point out that because change is more complex than ever to reach your goal you need to avoid what Malcolm Follos calls "cut, paste and modify" when really it is a "chance to reboot". David Walker and I look at messy, VUCA, complex problems in *The Art of Coping with Complexity*. When change is tricky to solve the temptation to do nothing or be seen to be doing something are both usually the worst options. Only with a fully rounded action plan and tackling the interdependencies can the outcome be positive. Michelle Brailsford in *Emergent Change Needed Urgently - Doing Change Differently in a VUCA World* also warns against tinkering – she urges more innovative, imaginative and possibly radical solutions – using all talent available to the organisation.

Which neatly brings us to the second thread.

2. People are your key

Trust, writes Julia Felton, "acts like a lubricant" and helps everyone pull together in the same direction. It is hard gained and easily lost so earning trust is vital in any change programme. She states purposeful communication with your audience is key and in *The Human Touch, Communicating So People Want To Change* Karen Dempster shows how important an impactful, consistent communication strategy is to help people feel good about their part in the future of the organisation rather than suffer what she alarmingly calls "change hangover". In *Bringing Visions and Strategy to Life* Malcolm has a compelling metaphor to show how successful leaders, rather than focusing on managing change, should be helping others have the "confidence that the future will be better than today".

One of the biggest jeopardies in change programmes is the failure to motivate the people who you rely on to enact your change. Karen highlights the role of communication to keep motivation high and John Hackett shows how work place self-esteem is determined by our level of understanding of how we make an impact. His framework in *Change Alchemy: Delivering Game-Changing Transformation That Sticks* integrates what he calls the organisational system – people, work design and conditions – to ensure an alignment. Simon Phillips widens influence to change to include all partners in *Stakeholder Engagement Revisited*. But, if that seems a daunting task, in order to not spread yourself thinly he shows how to target efforts for greatest impact.

And there is no escaping our own relationship with change – this is not something that 'others' do. We need to be 'Change Fit'. Resilience specialist Vanda North understands the coping strategies to manage modern life. In *Build Your Resilience For Work And Life In Just 8-Minutes A Day* she explains her proven *Mind Chi* technique so we all can have what she calls 'bounceability.' Cathy Summers offers us up a mirror and asks the tough question – are we proactive with changes in our own careers in *Managing Your Career During Change* and enables us to handle this personal change better.

It is worth reminding ourselves if we look back several years it is easier to recognise that we have always been on this change journey and we generally do learn from it – but perhaps not as fast as we could. We now know that reflective learning helps us learn faster, problem solve better and feel in more control. In my chapter *Why We Should All Invest Time In Reflective Learning* I make the case for this to be more normalised in learning organisations. But there is no escaping for many that constant change is stressful. And finally, this stress can overspill into conflict and in Angie Beeston's *Conflict Management – Managing Difficult Behaviours* she gives us a clear understanding of how to avoid this when our beliefs and attitudes are tested. She challenges us to understand our own mindset so we can manage tensions "are these behaviours difficult or just different?"

How you approach your need for change and engage the people who you rely on to make it a success is hard to get 'right'. This book gives a view on how to deal with some of the knotty change issues, and there is plenty of scope for Volume 2.

Nicky Carew

London

November 2017

community@thechangemakergroup.com

WHAT DOES A CHANGE MAKER LOOK LIKE?

By David Walker

Snapshot: In all aspects of life there is a conflict between appearance and reality. This is true of change makers too, where appearance or pre-conceptions are not a good predictor of actual behaviours. David Walker puts his tongue firmly in his cheek to explore the habits of change makers.

It's an important question. At The Change Maker Group we aim to create a legacy of Change Makers in whatever we do, supporting change in being self-sustaining for our clients. One of the challenges is being able to identify a Change Maker to allow us to support and nurture them and develop their skills.

People have an image of the story behind any personal label. Everyone knows that a geek is a 20-something, bespectacled man with long hair ("geeks" are just as likely to be female and/or older), a nurse is always a woman (10% of nurses in the UK are men..) and a refuse collector wears a flat cap and smokes woodbines (they don't).

These are all stereotypes, but we all have an image of the person that fulfils a particular role in society, politicians, media, movies, sport or whatever. Whilst groups of people have a perceived uniform, in truth compliance or non-compliance to the norm tells us little about the person.

But stereotyping a Change Maker is a bit more difficult.

Let's try a few dress styles. Will that help us work out what a Change Maker looks like?

- Pinstripe suit…"one is unable to say".
- Grungy jeans and Kurt Cobain T-shirt…"dunno mate".
- Twinset and pearls…"oh, no…".
- Long flowing dress and straw hat…"no way of knowing darling".

Point made I hope – image is a poor predictor of behaviour.

How will we ever assess what a Change Maker looks like? We might as well say that they look like Martians – two heads, tentacles, green with pink spots (remember stereotypes…)

So, there is no way of knowing what a Change Maker looks like then?

Apart from the obvious question of "does it matter what a change maker looks like?" (it doesn't), being a Change Maker is about how one acts, rather than how one looks. There is a human fixation about image, which overrides how a person is expected and/or perceived to act, whatever the reality.

For instance;

- My image of Martin Luther King is a man in a suit – he was definitely a Change Maker.
- Gandhi in his traditional Indian dress – definitely a Change Maker.
- Diana, Princess of Wales – a Change Maker.
- Supposedly scruffy Bob Geldof – a Change Maker.
- The Dalai Lama – a Change Maker.
- Bill Gates in his open neck shirt and jeans – Change Maker.

But one doesn't have to be famous to be a Change Maker, and it really doesn't matter about the physical appearance of a Change Maker. There are people in all of our lives that are Change Makers. In their own ways and without image stereotypes they display a series of traits:

- They care deeply about people.
- They believe that change can only come by engaging with people.
- They care passionately about their vision, and they strive to share that vision with colleagues, neighbours, classmates.
- They don't worry about status or competing opinions, they recognise that everyone is different and has their own personality, egos, issues and constraints; and people are people.
- They lead and get stuff done, and don't have to be the boss to be successful.

community@thechangemakergroup.com

And perhaps a few more. Being a Change Maker is a state of mind and a preference to action, working with people to help them be the best they can be.

The Change Maker Group has a lot of tools and techniques available to help identify and subsequently nurture and support Change Makers, but identification is predominately a sense of the behaviours displayed. The introverted "Quiet Leadership" principles deployed by some is as effective in delivering change as those people who exhibit more extrovert behaviours.

There is no need to have a stereotypical image of a Change Maker, and anyway one doesn't exist. Anyone can be a Change Maker, even our two-headed Martian.

David Walker is a programme management and change professional, with a broad background across business sectors and functions. He is also a qualified accountant, but contests that he is not boring. David lives in Northamptonshire with his family, is an avid rugby fan, is heavily involved in his local community, and writes the occasional pantomime.

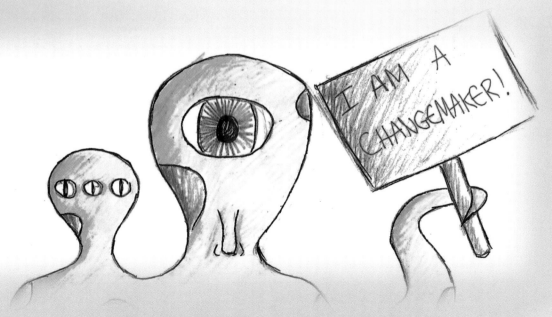

STRATEGIC CHANGE

There are times when you have to make change work for you and your organisation to deal with complex issues to stay ahead – but which way to go? Change Makers examine the issues and use their experience of working with organisations through change to point to what will make a difference.

community@thechangemakergroup.com

VISIONS, MISSIONS AND ALL THAT JAZZ

by Malcolm Follos

Snapshot: The Power of Purpose, what are Visions and Mission statements really for and who really cares? Malcolm Follos explores why we do what we do and gives us tips on how to create a great Vision statement.

A wise man once said 'when you are born you are given a brush – you can paint heaven or you can paint hell, the choice is yours, so choose well my friend.'

The insight contained in this neat quote is clear, we all need a higher purpose and a reason to be otherwise our life is just a drudge.

I often replay this quote when we get asked to help leaders and their teams look into the future and 'imagineer' a vision and mission for their team, function or organisation as a whole. I despair when I read the mind numbing, generic pap that often pass as a mission statement in some organisations. You know the sort that state they exist to deliver outstanding customer service, to deliver sustainable shareholder value, to ……who cares, really, who cares!

Clarity of purpose and having a compelling reason to work is one of the keys that can unlock the discretionary effort and this in turn is a source of hidden productivity in all organisations. It is amazing how much creativity and effort will be unleashed when we are working on something we believe is a great thing to do.

In this chapter we will explore the role a well thought through vision and mission can have on helping us all keep in mind the real purpose of why we do what we do and share some tips on how to create a great mission and vision.

The Trigger

For many leaders the chance to look into the future comes along when we are required to create, or to review and revise our strategy. In large organisations this is an annual ritual that usually precedes the budgets and can unfortunately often be an energy sapping, 'cut, paste and modify', template driven exercise that does nothing to enlighten the soul. However, for some leaders, usually those fairly new in post, or who feel a strong sense of ownership for their own area, it is a chance to 'reboot' themselves and their leadership teams and to lift their heads up from the operational treadmill and focus beyond the current issues horizon.

As such, reconnecting with your purpose can energise and help leaders co-create a future worth working towards.

Who Cares?

The desire to drop down into detail and to rush to develop action plans and financial budgets can be overwhelming and it has to be resisted until a clear and compelling vision of the future can be discussed, honed and developed. As the Cat in Lewis Carol's Alice in Wonderland so aptly said, and I paraphrase:

'If you do not know where you are going then any road will take you there'

A clear and compelling picture of where *'there'* is has to be the first step in any strategic journey.

It can be useful to remind ourselves who we create visions and missions for and what they want. In my view there are four key audiences for a vision and mission, they are:

Leaders and managers in your organisation – who need some guidance that the day-to-day decisions they are taking are correct in those important moments of truth; those moments when decisions have to be taken that matter.

Customers and consumers – who demand differentiation and want to know why they should deal with you and not your competitors and want some confidence that you are building towards a future that is in tune with their own values and aspirations.

Employees and recruits – who want to do meaningful work and to understand why what they do is worth doing. They also want to have the confidence in you as leaders that you are steering the organisation to a destination worth their efforts. Remember customers will never love a company until the employees love it first.

community@thechangemakergroup.com

Investors and stakeholders – who want to have confidence that the leadership have clarity of purpose and are creating a future they consider is worth investing in.

In thinking about your vision and mission it is well worth keeping these diverse audiences' in mind. A really good vision and mission will satisfy all four.

Definitions

At this point it is worth pausing and clarifying some nomenclature. I have found the words used is the strategic arena can be subject to many different interpretations – you will be surprised how many different types of answer I get to the simple question *'can you tell me what your strategy is?'* So let me be clear.

When I use the word *'mission'* I am talking about the purpose of your organisation, why you exist, your overall aim and why this matters. It acts as your 'Northern Star' that guides all the work you do and helps you recognise a distraction when one emerges.

One of the better mission statements I have seen in recent years was crafted initially as an advertising campaign for Pedigree Pet Foods and came from the CEO, otherwise known as the 'Top Dog'. It goes as follows:

'We're for Dogs. Some people are for the whales, some are for the trees, we're for dogs. The big ones; the little ones; the guardians; the comedians; the pure breeds; and the mutts. We're for walks, runs and romps. Digging, scratching, sniffing and fetching. We're for dog parks, dog doors and dog days. If there were an international holiday for dogs on which all dogs were universally recognised for the contribution to the quality of life on earth, we'd be for that too. Because we're for dogs, and we have spent the last 60 years working to make them as happy as they have made us. Dogs rule.'

It's a little bit long but nonetheless it's pretty neat!

When I use the word *'vision'* in the context of strategy I mean a picture of a destination worth arriving at, an ambition that is beyond our immediate horizon and one that is compelling and desirable to reach. It is important that this destination talks as much to the heart as it does the head, as I have come across far too many visions that are simply dull and boring, or alternatively are far too ambitious so they become de-motivating. As a top tip anything that promises to make others rich and successful while you and your people work hard is unlikely to inspire. There has to be something in it for everyone. Your vision should be granular enough to answer the questions where are we heading and how will we know when we have arrived?

How to Create a Great Vision and Mission

In recent years I have encouraged leadership teams to use props, sketches and pictures to represent their purpose and intent. This stimulates a different quality of debate that I find is necessary to break free from the prevailing mind-set and constraints of the often brutal current reality.

The props metaphor has produced some really interesting results over the years. I simply ask participants to bring along something that for them represents what the organisation is like now and also something that represents for them what they would like the organisation to be in the future.

For example, I had one director bring along a Sat Nav to represent the now and an old fashioned car roadmap to represent the future. At first glance this looked odd? When it was explained it became clear, the Sat Nav is a central control tool, it recommends the direction and if you deviate it will tell you immediately to get back on course. The car roadmap however lays out many possibilities and you can collaborate and agree the journey you want to take. The fast but dull motorway, or the scenic but usually slower country lane. The message on the prevailing culture was not lost on the leadership team and it sparked a lively debate about what culture they needed to succeed with their purpose.

The sketch metaphor can also produce some interesting insights. In this I ask the team to work in smaller groups and come up with a poster that will attract new recruits to the organisation they want to create. The poster can have headlines and sketches that bring to life their organisation in a way that words alone will struggle to convey. Again the discussions that ensue are at a different level than the usual budget setting session will create as people can be far more expressive with pictures than they can be with words alone.

Once a collective view of the future is agreed I leave this alone and let this settle before attempting to craft a set of words that match these insights. Then I suggest we start with a headline, slogan or motto that incorporates what we are really all about, our 'We're for Dogs' equivalent. Honda has 'Dare to Dream'; Google 'Don't be evil'; British Airways 'To Fly to Serve; etc.

What is yours?

community@thechangemakergroup.com

Then when a headline exists set about describing why you exist and where you are heading, in a way that is compelling, concise and clear. This will take several iterations to get right but the honing and refining is worth the effort as it is imperative all members of the leadership team can explain what the resulting words mean in a way that they understand, believe and can therefore commit to.

How they say what they say is far more important than what they actually say!

Now What and So What?

Your *mission* will give clarity of purpose and your *vision* will give clarity of destination. The next step in the process is to develop a strategic storyboard that shows the journey from now to the future and then engage everyone in the organisation with this work.

The best way to do this is to tell a story and this is the subject of the next chapter in this book.

Malcolm Follos is a proven specialist in working with leaders and their teams around the world. He helps leaders engage human performance to deliver strategically significant results. He is an accomplished management consultant, executive coach, leadership team facilitator, keynote conference speaker, author and renowned trainer. He is also a dance teacher with a mad as a box of frogs Springer Spaniel to walk every 4 hours!

Bringing Vision and Strategy to Life

by Malcolm Follos

Snapshot: A strategy should be a compelling, living story and should be highly visible within an organisation, not buried away in a deck of slides and spreadsheets. Malcolm Follos helps you discover how to make this so.

Far too many vision statements and accompanying strategy presentations put people to sleep. Leaders find them difficult to present and participants find them even more difficult to listen to. They are full of corporate and management speak that fails to engage the heart as well as the head of the people they are developed by and for. Enough of this nonsense. This annual ritual has to stop.

What people want to hear is their leaders describing the future in a way that gives them the confidence that the future will be better than today and will enable them to contribute, and to some extent shape their own destiny. Leaders want this too, so all that is missing is the will to break a well-embedded corporate ritual and a new strategy process designed to engage the heart as well as the head. This is what we have been working on over the last couple of years and what we can offer to organisations wanting to breathe new life into their strategy process.

Our process encourages leaders to 'dream the impossible dream'. We help leaders let their imagination soar. We encourage them to draw their vision as a composite picture, one that is colourful, desirable and shows a future destination worth getting out of bed each day for. When this is formed then, and only then, do we introduce the rational reality on which all future strategies have to be based if they are to succeed. Once the destination is known amazingly the starting point becomes a lot clearer too. Current challenges and issues

community@thechangemakergroup.com

have the strategic perspective necessary to help leaders extend their thinking horizon and begin to focus on the journey that lies ahead.

Put simply a vision is a destination worth arriving at. One that transcends current reality and is beyond the current issues horizon. A great vision should be uplifting and reflective of the primary purpose of the organisation. "*To make sustainable living common place*" says Unilever; "*To refresh the world*" says Coca-Cola and "*To become the most creative organisation in the world*" says the BBC; "*To save and improve lives*" says NHS Blood & Transplant. All of these examples are designed to remind everyone that there is something worth doing and the destination is worth all their effort.

A strategy is simply answering the question – how are we going to get there and what do we need to do if we are to succeed along the way?

We find this is best developed as a story. A story that can be drawn onto a large strategic journey storyboard, clearly showing the journey into the future, highlighting the key achievements along the way; the headwinds you will have to face; the tailwinds that will blow you along; all the opportunities; potential distractions; and risks that will give the story its flavour and substance.

This picture shows a European CEO sharing their strategic storyboard with the heads of business and functional leaders. We find leaders enjoy creating and then telling these stories and as a result they appear enthusiastic and credible, two leadership attributes that all too often get lost in a corporate power point presentation. Also, managers listening find the story easy to remember and re-tell, as they cascade the message into  their areas and departments. Our strategic storyboard process encourages everyone listening to participate with comments, builds and suggestions on what this story means for them in their day-to-day activity, thereby creating the elusive 'golden thread' linking day-to-day activity to strategic intent.

Strategy as a Little Black Dress

To create a great story does however require a good imagination and we use metaphors as stimuli for creative thought throughout our sessions. This metaphor helps orientate the leaders and gets the brain working.

Coco Chanel is credited with the creation of one of the great designs of the twentieth century, the 'Little Black Dress'. The lessons from this timeless creation for people embarking on the art of crafting a strategy are profound. Taking its inspiration from the uniforms of domestic help in 1920's Paris, it quickly established itself as a design of astonishing endurance in the notoriously fickle world of women's fashion.

Anyone seeking to understand the qualities of a well-designed business strategy would do well to begin by understanding the enduring allure of Chanel's design. There are three key lessons this design can teach those who seek to craft strategy for their organisation.

Lesson #1 – Make your strategy simple yet elegant – The most striking aspect of the design of the 'Little Black Dress' is its stark simplicity. It does not come in numerous colours instead it offers a black canvas which its wearer tailors to the function in hand – add heels and pearls to dress up, a bright scarf and flats to dress casual. The possibilities are endless.

The same can be said of a well-crafted organisational strategy. It should be parsimonious, in that it lacks nothing essential, yet contains nothing extraneous. It will provide direction and clarity of purpose yet it can be shaped to suit the challenges faced by different geographies, functions and departments within. The basic design is fixed but the excitement and colour can be added to suit the situation and tailor the fit for all.

Lesson #2 – Your strategy should be timeless & popular – The 'Little Black Dress' has remained unchallenged in the ultimate of faddish fields for almost 100 years! Most women have one in their wardrobe and this is simply astonishing. The secret could lie in the transformational properties that lie within the design. When a woman slips into her 'Little Black Dress' she becomes more of the woman she aspires to be, she is elevated and feels good. The fabric flows and the colours are flattering and the outcome is stunning.

Can the same be said when managers and leaders leave the room after crafting their strategy I wonder? A great test of any strategy is to ask; how does this strategy make you feel? If the

community@thechangemakergroup.com

response is along the lines of 'the beatings will continue until the morale improves!' then perhaps more work is needed.

A great strategy should engender excitement and pride, emotions that are often missing from far too many boardrooms in my humble opinion. A focus on what makes the organisation great and enduring will help focus the mind and a challenge to everyone to contribute their own personal adornments to the strategy to make it represent their own will help with engagement and alignment.

Lesson #3 – Your strategy should create openings for new adventures – Like the '*Little Black Dress*' a great strategy is a stepping off point for new adventures. It should recognise and fit with existing reality, but not be constrained by it. It should look beyond the current issues horizon towards a bright, compelling and attractive future that makes people look forward to the journey ahead.

Strategic stories should echo the familiar whilst at the same time providing the chance to script some new stories that are fresh and exciting. Your strategic story should make people feel confident, open to new adventures and ready to find something special just around the corner.

If a '*Little Black Dress*' can do this why can't your business strategy?

(Thanks to 'Strategy Bites Back – Mintzberg, Ahlstrand, Lampel and Jeanne Liedtka' for this metaphor)

In this short chapter we have explored some simple principles, lessons and techniques designed to help bring your vision and strategy to life in a way that can engage the whole organisation.

The key challenge we find is to break the 'cut and paste' cycle that exists in so many organisations where last year's strategic slide deck is brought out, a few amendments are made to reflect current reality and some latest views from the top and the focus quickly shifts to the budgets and spreadsheets so the poker game that is the budget setting process can commence in earnest.

This nonsense has to stop!

Malcolm Follos is a proven specialist in working with leaders and their teams around the world. He helps leaders engage human performance to deliver strategically significant results. He is an accomplished management consultant, executive coach, leadership team facilitator, keynote conference speaker, author and renowned trainer. He is also a dance teacher with a mad as a box of frogs Springer Spaniel to walk every 4 hours!

community@thechangemakergroup.com

ESTABLISH SOLID FOUNDATIONS FOR POSITIVE CULTURE AND CHANGE

by Richard Flewitt

Snapshot: What does the core of your organisation need to look and feel like before you can experience positive, authentic and successful change? Richard Flewitt has interviewed leaders from major UK brands to discover the essential ingredients.

I have a hypothesis that I'd like share with leaders and business owners... but before I do, some context will give you an insight to my reasoning and approach.

It is my belief that all public and private sector organisations as well as businesses of all sizes operate within a culture, even if there is only one person in the business. Customers, suppliers, colleagues and employees all have a sense of that culture, whether it has been articulated or not and, to varying degrees, there is a direct correlation between the culture and the success or failure of change activities within an organisation or business.

Just imagine for a moment that every single employee is enthusing about your services or products at every opportunity because they totally believe in your organisation and what you stand for. They understand and agree with your mission and can see how they are part of a business that is making a positive difference at some level. Not only are they happier at work and therefore less likely to want to leave or take an unwarranted 'sickie', they do whatever they can to support your change agenda and strategic decisions in order to ensure that your company thrives. Your customers see and feel this enthusiasm at all levels pre and post sales/service delivery and therefore associate your brand with this positive culture.

Now consider the alternative scenario ...... your employees are not particularly engaged by what you do, why you do it and how you do it; they simply turn up each day, do their work adequately and efficiently, take their money and go home. They are not especially enthusiastic at work, they feel little loyalty to you, your desire for change or your strategy. They are happy to keep turning up as long as you continue to pay them. They do not make good advocates when talking about your company to customers or acquaintances because they don't really care. They forget about work as soon as they walk out of the door. Customers are still engaged to an extent because your products are priced competitively, or your service supply is the norm for them but when it is time for their next requirement they have no emotional reason to remember you or desire to engage with you again.

Which option would you prefer?

By developing a positive and purposeful culture, then making sure it is embodied by every individual across your organisation you will build solid foundations on which to create positive change and a culture that will drive sustainable success. Employee engagement and retention will improve saving you money on expensive recruitment campaigns. Customers will recognise your brand as being synonymous with a friendly, positive and caring service; increasing both customer loyalty and referrals.

"The brands that will thrive in the coming years are the ones that have a purpose beyond profit."

Richard Branson

Over the last twelve months I have interviewed leaders from some of the UK's most established brands in order to test my hypothesis, understand their thoughts around company culture and how the concept of purpose has a place in business. Extracts from some of those interviews will support my thinking and give you an insight into the future of business and leadership.

'*Brand Essence* ' is a favourite term of mine as I believe that it captures the *feeling* that underpins the culture of a company or organisation. It gives customers, employees and stakeholders a sense of what the brand is all about, informs the change process and ultimately, helps to inform whether you are the right company to buy from, work for or do business with. As Mark Sears, former Head of Brand Strategy at Virgin says,

"Ninety percent of a brand is about what it is like beneath the surface, only ten percent about what it looks like"

So what exactly is the 'essence' of a brand, how does it have an impact on our success?

When you visit a shop, office or factory that you haven't been to before and meet the people there, you get an instinctive feeling pretty quickly as to whether you get a good feeling about them, whether you like them and feel comfortable there. Have you noticed how you know that you can buy the same service or products from a range of companies, yet you are drawn to one particular provider by a 'gut feeling' that tells you the company that stands out for you. That feeling - the fluffy, intangible sense that is really difficult to explain in words is, in fact, the 'essence' of the brand. Just imagine how powerful it would be if you could articulate that feeling in tangible words that you can use in marketing and recruitment to attract and retain the right customers and employees for your business.

This is precisely what some big brands such as John Lewis and Virgin have done. The essence of their brand has become fundamental to the culture of the organisation, informing change and key strategic decisions at every level of operation.

As Paula Nickolds, MD of John Lewis retail told me,

John Lewis

"We're not 150 years old by accident – in order to evolve and continue to secure a brand like we have, I think it owes more to the culture and the people than it ever does the MD, or the decisions being made by the board"

John Lewis is a unique organisation that still lives by its original constitution as laid out by Stephen Lewis, son of the original founder, John Lewis. 'Principle One' of that constitution is that the purpose of the organisation is to 'provide worthwhile and satisfying employment for partners in a successful business'. This purpose is fundamental to the culture today and is considered whenever the executive team are managing change. Paula Nickolds explains,

"We don't just decide to change something because it will be more profitable. We decide to change it because we ask three things: Does it produce a better customer proposition, is it likely to be more financially rewarding, and is it going to generate something that is more satisfying and fulfilling for our partner population"

Purpose in popular business terminology translates to WHY; Your WHY is your purpose, the reason you and your people get up in the morning and come to work. Within companies who articulate and openly share their purpose, the WHY is the reason that employees are enthusiastic, and go the extra mile to help them with innovative and creative ideas.

You may be aware of the leadership guru, Simon Sinek who's popular

Ted talk and website, *Start with Why* explains how purpose sits at the heart of every successful business.

Sinek uses consumer technology giant, Apple, whilst under the leadership of Steve Jobs as an example. At that time Apple's mission statement was to

 'Make a contribution to the world by making tools for the mind that advance humankind'

This is an excellent example of a WHY, or purpose, that is really 'big picture' and gives employees and customers an insight into the reason behind the culture of the organisation. Ultimately it is my belief that all companies have a deeper purpose beyond making profit. Products and services are created to make other people's lives better, healthier, richer or happier in some way.

Many, many companies and organisations do not take the time to step back from the day-to-day business in order to discover and articulate this, but it exists nonetheless. To this point I absolutely agree with Sinek that your WHY should be is at the centre of everything you do. If you have an authentic purpose, you can share it with potential employees to attract like-minded people and share it with customers to attract more loyalty – just as in the John Lewis model.

From my research I have discovered that, in order to be unique in your market and articulate the core essence of your brand, having a WHY is not enough. There is another element. Imagine for me if you will, two accountancy companies who have identical offices on the same high street. You visit their websites and discover that they proclaim an identical mission or purpose for their being in business. You decide to make appointments to visit both practices and discover that, in reality, the two practices 'feel' totally different. You really like the feel and approach of one while the other repels you in some way.

Yet they both state an identical purpose that underpins the direction and style of their business...

A common thread from the interviews I have carried out so far suggests strongly that your people are a key element to your culture, and therefore the success of your future. Given that the people within an organisation have been recruited by the business owner or under guidance of the executive team, I suggest that the other element at play when determining the core essence of the brand is the element I call the WHO.

The John Lewis partnership in 2017 would not be what it is without an element of the characteristics and values of its founders pervading its culture. Apple would not have been the same organisation without the key characteristics and values of Steve Jobs driving the style of the business towards achieving their admirable mission. Interestingly, under the most recent executive team, Apple does not publish a mission statement as such on their website. They reportedly end all press releases with the following statement that is as near to a mission as I can find:

'Apple is committed to bringing the best personal computing experience to students, educators, creative professionals and consumers around the world through its innovative hardware, software and Internet offerings.'

To me this does not encompass an ethos that underpins the brand and informs customers and employees; it is not 'big picture' or inspirational in the way that the former mission statement under the leadership of Jobs was. Could the fact that the big picture mission is missing affect the core of the business and explain the consumer confusion around the brand today?

All the leaders I have spoken to in my research place their people at the top of their priority list when considering culture and longevity within their organisation. My conclusion, therefore, is that in addition to your focus on purpose or your WHY, your WHO, the key characteristics that drive the nature of how you operate and interact with people, sits right in the centre of your organisation determining its culture and Brand Essence.

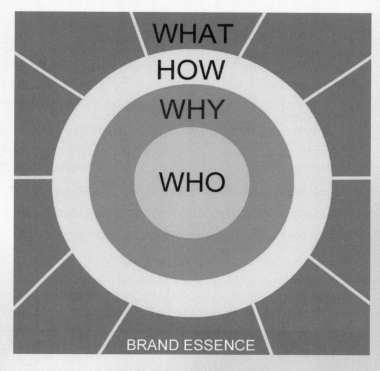

Your WHO will usually be 'held' by your CEO/MD or executive leadership team and represents the characteristics that define who you are as a company. Your WHO is unique to you, as leaders and business owners, because it is about your people - at all levels of the company, and defines your style of operation; are you a company who acts in a determined, passionate, goal-oriented style, or are you more grounded, connected and creative in your approach?

If you are not attracting the right people by sharing your WHY and WHO, your authentic brand essence, there is a really good chance that your culture as perceived by customers is not a true representation of your mission and values. You therefore attract the wrong customers, they buy less or not at all, employee motivation goes down and the spiral continues. Turn this around so that everybody is involved and 'singing from the same sheet', change programs are aligned with the company ethos, you attract customers who agree, they spend more, profits rise, staff are more motivated and the spiral goes the other way.

When you take the time to discover your authentic brand essence and embody it across your organisation it will be the foundation of all future change and success. Whether that success for you is about turnover and profit or about changing the world, when your people are on-board and share an enthusiasm and belief for your purpose, the success will take care of itself. For a great example and case study have a look at Buurtzorg[1] in the Netherlands who have revolutionised the care industry by improving the level of care to clients while also giving a much higher level of responsibility and autonomy to the nurses it employs.

In the UK a company that has been putting its people first for decades is Timpsons.

" It would be very sad if going to work was not fun. A lot of the stuff we do is actually quite fun. Why do you work for an organisation? Because you enjoy it and take pride in what it does... and you're there with like-minded people. It's sense of community."

John Timpson, Chairman of Timpson Group

To help create this ethos John Timpson speaks of the importance around recruiting people with the right attitudes and mind-set. All employees attend a residential training day after completing their 3-month probationary period, the main intention being to explain and embody the culture. Timpson also talks about an 'upside down pyramid' structure in which the front-line staff are at the top of the pyramid being supported by everybody else below. The board and executive team are at the bottom forming the solid foundations to support everybody above them. 'You can teach skills but you can't teach attitude' is a phrase that is shared by both Timpson and Center Parc's CEO, Martin Dalby.

Dalby, also speaks very warmly and passionately about the culture that has evolved at the company since 1987 describing the 7,500 strong work-force as a family and team who all work together towards the same shared mission. Whilst he acknowledges that profit is an essential measure of success for the business and its shareholders, he firmly believes that the culture and people at Center Parcs sit centre stage:

"Creating success is done through the less tangible aspects of the business. When we get the people right, the customer service right, the quality of the

community@thechangemakergroup.com

facilities right and the right essence around the brand, we know that the financial success will come"

Martin Dalby, CEO, Center Parcs

So how can you, as leaders, articulate your company essence to give both customers and colleagues a deeper insight into your organisation?

I, nor anyone else working around the change agenda, is suggesting that you can introduce a purpose-lead approach to culture and change overnight. Trust and communication are required in both directions and, as with any shift in culture the two magic ingredients are intention and time. The time it takes to establish a positive and purposeful culture is one of the main blocks that prevents leaders from doing it. As John Timpson acknowledges, consistency and perseverance is also playing a part:

"It took five years for the area management team to accept that this was the right way to run the business. Most of them pretended they agreed with me then went off and told everyone what to do. One of my rules is that no one is allowed to tell anyone what to do - you don't issue orders. You just don't run a business like that."

John Timpson, Chairman of Timpson Group

My invitation to leaders and business owners is to consider how you might set out on this road by first making the time to discover and articulate the core essence of your brand. Explore and experiment with possibilities around how you can engage more openly with your people, creating a culture in which your purpose known, understood and shared by all stakeholders.

A simple 3-step approach will help you to put this in place:

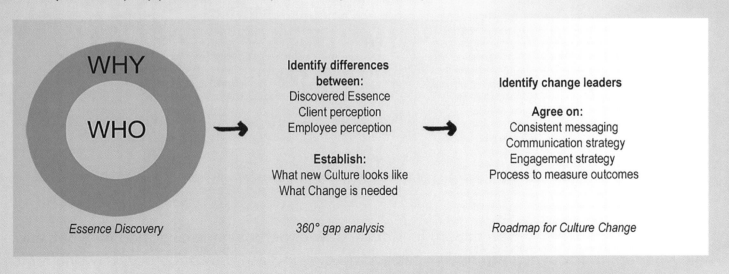

Step 1 – Take time to gain absolute clarity around your essence, purpose and core characteristics. From this discovered 'brand essence' create mission and value statements that represent the truth of who you are and why you do what you do. Together, these elements will establish firm foundations on which to build a truly positive and authentic culture.

Step 2 – Carry out a comprehensive 360° analysis comparing your new desired culture with the present perceived culture of both customers and of employees. This will highlight the differences, and therefore inform changes that are needed for you to move forwards positively and inclusively.

Step 3 – Create a tangible plan mapping out the necessary changes and agree on a practical timeline for embedding change, remembering that these activities are all in addition to the day job. Working with members of your current team or with carefully selected specialists be sure to communicate at every step of the way with all your employees - take them on the journey with you. This means listening as well as broadcasting, so within your change plan facilitate the time to hear feedback and suggestions from everyone AND make sure you also respond.

Developing a truly positive and purposeful culture will take time and may well present you with some difficult challenges. However, the time and effort you invest now will create benefits across your organisation for many years to come. Your new culture will get your whole team 'on-side' and fully align through all key activities that result in change, whether HR, recruitment, employee engagement, branding, marketing or sales.

   Your CEO and leadership team embody the core essence in all activities and communications - listening to and valuing opinions from every level of the company.

   Your sales and marketing people use key words that represent the company essence to attract the right customers who are most likely to buy and value your services from the outset,

   Your HR team include your company essence in the recruitment process and training programmes, making sure that all employees are aligned and believe in what you are doing

   Your R & D team create new products and services that align with your essence so that every employee believes in them and customers see them as belonging to your brand.

Of course, you also need to have systems and processes in place to ensure that the company is run efficiently, productively and profitably. Remember though that it is people who set up

community@thechangemakergroup.com

and run those systems, and it is people who will ultimately determine whether you are successful or not. If all those people are totally on-board with your purpose, ethos and values they will want you to succeed and will do whatever they can to help you.

To my hypothesis......

The essence of a brand sits at the heart of a purposeful and positive culture. If, as leaders, we know our WHY, our authentic core purpose, and if we can articulate our WHO, the key characteristics that drive our style and approach to business, it is very likely that we will attract like-minded people who truly understand us. With the right people on-board who buy into our culture, the essence will be embodied and flow throughout the business. As a result, the success of change programs, and indeed the success of the organisation as a whole is more likely to be optimised.

I took the opportunity to present this statement to all my interviewees, one of which was Will Wakefield, the CEO of the YMCA in Nottingham.

"We need to communicate very early on why we do what we do, and then how we do it. It is absolutely critical that we get the right people on board who share our culture"

Will Wakefield, YMCA

The organisation has enjoyed increased turnover of 20% year on year under his leadership taking it from less than £500,000 to over £7 million per annum. Will believes that developing a positive culture that everybody now feels part of played a crucial part in this success. In order to achieve this, their purpose and values are embedded into the recruitment process which includes a 3-day interview to ensure that new recruits are a good fit. The results speak for themselves.

Paula Nickolds was also in agreement, explaining to me that the essence of John Lewis forms the foundations that underpin activities across the whole organisation:

"It's easier to evolve and change, and there'll be more requirement for this in the future if you have a really clear purpose and reason for being and if you're absolutely clear about what your golden thread is, it helps you. It isn't a hindrance to change, it helps you because it's a kind of guiding, divining rod. It helps you to evolve and embrace the change that you need to survive"

Martin Dalby is very confident that by choosing the right people who are a match with the Center Parcs essence, then continually working hard to embody this culture across all its sites, the result will be evident:

"I'd like to think that if you walk into one of our parks and talk to any of our employees they would be able to understand and articulate what Center Parcs is all about. They might not use the right words or marketing jargon, but they would talk to you about the place where families can go, get back to nature and create memories."

Former Head of Brand at Virgin, Mark Sears, also agrees:

"You're not just on the right lines here, you're doing vital work within organisations now because organisations need to change. More than ever before we are faced with deep uncertainty in our world – there are really big issues that we need to solve as a society. I see brands as a really big cog in that and brands therefore have a responsibility towards their own purpose, towards doing something that is deeper than just earning cash for their shareholders. That means having a purpose, embodying that in their essence and supporting their people to thrive."

The conclusion that I am coming to during this research exercise is that my hypothesis is right, up to a point, for business in the early 21st century. While there are a few examples such as Buurtzorg in the Netherlands and Haier[2] in China who have fully embraced this new way of working, the overall consensus is more cautious. Purpose and people are essential elements to positive and successful culture and change, but shareholders of early 21st Century organisations still want and need to see a level of more traditional structure, accountability and hierarchy; i.e. The bottom line. There is definitely a shift, and the starting point for those who want to begin the journey is to discover and articulate their authentic core essence.

"This stuff is gold dust now for leaders in the 21st Century because without it brands can't play the role that they need to play – and they have to step up"

Mark Sears

I will leave the final word on whether this newer, more inclusive and positive way of working is right for 21st century businesses to Paula Nickolds:

"Do you know what, it's just a lot more fun. It's a lot more enjoyable way of being involved in a business. Culturally it creates a sense of personal satisfaction that I think it is really difficult to get in the same way in a traditional organisation. If you think of Maslow's hierarchy of needs, all of us at our core, once we're fed and watered and have a roof over our heads need a sense of purpose in life and it's an incredible way of getting one."

community@thechangemakergroup.com

[1] Read more on the Buurtzorg organisational structure and culture here: https://www.buurtzorg.com/about-us/

[2] Haier is a white goods manufacturer that operates numerous self-managed teams including employees from all levels of the company to guide strategic decisions and has abolished all levels of middle management. http://www.haier.net/en/about_haier/Leadership/introduction/

Richard Flewitt has witnessed the actions and attitudes of a variety of senior leaders, businesses and organisations throughout his varied career spanning TV journalism, corporate messaging and leadership training. Richard has a particular focus on the 'why' that sits behind the actions and attitudes that drive people, particularly in business and has amassed powerful insights into the future world of work, and corporate culture.

Emergent Change Needed Urgently : Doing Change Differently in a VUCA World

by Michelle Brailsford

> Snapshot: Michelle Brailsford challenges you with some new and provocative ways to think about change differently!

In the midst of incredible complexity, many leaders are still trying to lead change using management tools that are no longer relevant and change management approaches that only worked when change was 'predictable'. It's become a trendy managerial acronym: VUCA, short for *volatility, uncertainty, complexity,* and *ambiguity* but the reality is, in today's VUCA world, there are no 'right answers'. In a world where the future isn't predictable, we need to start using new tools and novel approaches.

Even as knowledge, resources, and tools for effective change have evolved, the one thing that has not changed is how many individuals, coaches, and organisations approach change. Despite numerous studies showing that an understanding of how our minds function helps us make better behaviour change, few coaches are applying what we know about mind set.

Despite popular books like *Switch: How to Change Things When Change Is Hard,* written by Chip and Dan Heath[1], which espouses a new way to do change that really works, few individuals, coaches, and organisations focus equally on *hearts* and *minds.*

And with all the recent talk about Lean, Scrum, and Agile, few case studies exist showing how application of these concepts helped drive change.

Doing Change Differently: Consider Open Source

Leaders must change the way they think about effectively inspiring change and transforming organisations. Many of our Leaders hold an 'old school' attitude about change, viewing it as a process to be managed from the top. But the latest thinking is around Open Sourced Change.

community@thechangemakergroup.com

I'll steal some terminology from software development to make my point. Most Leaders believe that change should be managed using the Cathedral model. This terminology comes from an essay written about software engineering methods, based on observations of the Linux development process and experiences managing an open source project, called fetchmail. It examined the struggle between top-down and bottom-up design.

The *Cathedral* model is a top-down mode where access to code is restricted, and the code is only available with each software release. Many organisational Leaders still feel that change needs to be controlled from the top down and that access to the change process needs to be limited, restricted and closed to all but an elite few including the Senior Leadership Team and the PMO (Project Management Office).

The Cathedral and the Bazaar: Musings on Linux and Open Source by an Accidental Revolutionary is an essay, and later a book, by Eric S. Raymond. The essay was first presented by the author at the *Linux Kongress* on May 27, 1997 in Würzburg and was published as part of the book in 1999.

Contrast this model with the *Bazaar* model, in which the code is developed over the internet in view of the public. Few changes are 'open sourced' (Bazaar model) or worked on in full view of the public, allowing all key stakeholders to participate. And the impact is that much change feels 'forced' upon the stakeholders. The numerous articles about 'how to overcome resistance' are proof that top down change creates conditions in which employees feel disconnected and disengaged.

The most common response, whether they believe the changes to be well founded or no, is to resist! The 'old school' way of thinking is to expect resistance and to plan for it from the start of the change management programme to allow you to effectively manage objections. The new, emergent way of thinking looks for ways to make change a collective effort.

Most leaders are familiar with what Open Source looks like in the software industry. Open source refers to a computer program in which the source code is available to the general public for use and/or modification from its original design. Open-source code is typically a collaborative effort where programmers improve upon the source code and share the changes within the community so that other members can help improve it further and all can benefit.

Most leaders are also familiar with Wikipedia, the free online encyclopaedia, created and edited by volunteers around the world and hosted by the Wikimedia Foundation. And all will be familiar with the benefits that organisations like Linux and Wikipedia derive by working open sourced.

Open Source approaches provide unique benefits such as:

* Inclusion of people with expertise who wouldn't otherwise have been included
* Free access to that expertise
* Diversity of perspectives
* Ability to update and improve in real time
* Greater likelihood of commitment to change

So why don't they apply Open Source to organisational change?

Some forward thinking organisational Leaders are beginning to do change using an Open Source (Bazaar) model, but they are few and far between. The inclusion of people in the change process who haven't studied strategy or project management scares most Leaders. The inclusion of a diverse range of perspectives is believed to slow down the process. Providing access to strategic plans also scares Leaders; they are afraid the competition may get hold of insider information.

However, we know that fresh eyes and different perspectives create better solutions. Scott Page has collected evidence that prove the benefits of diversity in his thought-provoking book, *The Difference: How the Power of Diversity Creates Better Groups, Firms, Schools, and Societies*[2]. And I believe that if we believe people can be trusted, they will behave in a trustworthy manner. So, the cost(s) are far outweighed by the benefits that include agility and commitment.

> *Leaders need to believe that change should be 'open sourced'. It is one of the vital mind shifts that is must happen before any organisation can adopt doing Change in an Emergent way.*

Thinking about Change Differently: Consider Holacracy ©

According to Holacracy.org, Holacracy is "a comprehensive practice for structuring, governing, and running an organisation. It replaces today's top-down predict-and-control paradigm with a new way of achieving control by distributing power". It is a new "operating system" that installs rapid evolution in the core processes of an organisation.

Rapid evolution? Sounds like change!

Online USA shoe retailer Zappos began a transition to Holacracy in 2013. They shifted to this model in order to create a process that allows everyone in the organisation to make changes and feel empowered to innovate.

Staff self-manage to the benefit of the greater 'whole' and move between groups or 'circles' to get things done.

Holacracy gives every single employee the opportunity to make changes if they think there's a newer or better way of doing something.

Employees with a suggestion for how to change a process don't have to go through a chain of command to get an idea in front of a wider audience.

But must organisations become Holacracies in order to drive new levels of involvement? Or can they simply change the culture inside their organisations so that change isn't Leader led?

Organisations can adopt the philosophy of Holacracy without swallowing all of the practices whole. This philosophy includes:

- Holacracy replaces the traditional hierarchy with a series of interconnected but autonomous teams ("circles")

- Rapid Iterations Replace Big Re-organisations

- Processing tension inside an organisation; tension has a place to go, where it will get processed quickly and effectively into organisational evolution

When people in the organisation sense tension, every tension they experience has a place to go, where it will get processed quickly and effectively into organisational evolution

Adopting new paradigms about distributed power ensures that we are engaging with people's brains differently. Instead of evoking a 'fight or flight' response, brains can be nudged into a 'tend and befriend' or towards state; a state of tending or taking care of each other in times of change, a state where we befriend those around us so that change is social and collaborative.

These new paradigms help stakeholders navigate the social world in the workplace so they can make better contributions.

Leaders need to believe that a new 'operating system' enabling change to be done better is possible. It is one of the vital mind shifts that is must happen before any organisation can adopt doing Change in an Emergent way.

Thinking about Change Differently: Change that Isn't Leader Led

In a famous HBR article, 'The 4 Things Successful Change Leaders Do'[3], the author writes,

'The leadership of the change effort can't end with the top team, the top 100 managers, or the top 1,000 managers. It should be an all-hands-on-deck engagement. The change leader must signal that enterprise-wide transformation will be a collective effort, with accountability distributed throughout the organisation.'

Change cannot simply be relegated to an elite team.

In the past, change has been 'managed' through a Change Programme. According to Wikipedia, 'Change management (CM) refers to any approach to transitioning individuals, teams and organisations using methods intended to re-direct the use of resources, business process, budget allocations, or other modes of operation that significantly reshape a company or organisation'.

Most change is still being 'managed' using a top down or PMO driven approach. Leadership teams deploy detailed plans for their change initiative to help employees understand what they need to do. PMO offices use formulas to calculate the ROI of change management, e.g. the amount of project benefits dependent on adoption and usage, and track changes in a linear fashion. Managers base these plans on change management principals found in methods such as Kotter's Eight-step process[4] or the ADKAR model[5] (Awareness of the need for change. Desire to make the change happen. Knowledge about how to change. Ability to implement new skills and behaviours. Reinforcement to retain the change once it has been made.)

The problem with this programmatic approach to change is that "leader-owned" implementation plans create a workforce that is sitting around waiting to be told what to do. At best leaders may get compliance versus true commitment to the change. At worst, leaders may get resistance. When cascaded down from the top, there is no guarantee that stakeholders will understand or go along with the prescribed changes. And the top-down approach fails to tap into the creativity and wisdom embedded across the organisation. This programmatic approach to change assumes that change is logic or rational; we know it isn't! The failure of most organisational change, I believe, is down to the single-minded focus on

community@thechangemakergroup.com

cost-benefit analysis or efficiency, emphasing benefits derived and shareholder value achieved. But shareholder value isn't the only measure of performance.

What about a cost-benefit analysis from a human perspective, focusing on issues such as positive emotional state of the employees?

What about adopting an 'all-hands-on-deck' engagement strategy that creates a wave of positive emotions around change?

What about creating change that is exciting instead of change that is resisted?

> *Leaders need to believe that change should be stakeholder led, not Leader led. It is one of the vital mind shifts that is must happen before any organisation can adopt doing Change in an Emergent way.*

Thinking about Change Differently: Change Management Platforms

In their 2014 McKinsey article, *Build a Change Platform, not a Change Program*[6], Authors Gary Hamel and Michele Zanini advocate for organisations creating a level playing field that enables everyone in the organisation to put forward their ideas to help launch change. They recognise that when it comes to change, full voices truly make superior choices. Effective change comes about when organisations build ways in which everyone can contribute ideas and drive change forward, when they can bring their Hearts and Minds to the party.

What the VUCA world needs is more bottom-up, spontaneous change sparked by the efforts of frontline activists but most organisations don't provide a platform to enable that to happen. How would organisations enable this type of change? They would place less emphasis on building PMO offices and more on building self-organising change communities that identify, experiment, and eventually scale new initiatives. They would build more Change Platforms. In their famous article, Gary Hamel and Michele Zanini suggest three shifts in approach:

> Push responsibility for initiating change down and across the organisation. Allow a group of Internal activists to drive grassroots change movements.

> Push responsibility for the "how" to everyone in the organisation. Instead of appointing a task force of senior leaders, invite the entire firm to a hackathon.

> Encourage constant experimentation. Generate a portfolio of experiments that can be conducted locally to help prove or disprove a hypothesis.

Leaders need to create an environment where change can happen anywhere -and at any time - and inspiring everyone, at every level to perform a change role. It is the vital behavioural shift that must happen in order for an organisation to adopt doing Change in an Emergent way.

Doing Change Differently: Leveraging all the Resources Inside the System

As we know, many change efforts fail to deliver the hoped for results.

Some highlights from the study, the 2013 Change and Communication ROI Survey, which involved 276 large and midsize organisations from North America, Europe and Asia:

> Employers felt 55% of change management initiatives met initial objectives, but only 25% felt gains were sustained over time.

> 87% of respondents trained their managers to "manage change," but only (a dismal) 22% felt the training was actually effective.

> 68% of senior managers said they're "getting the message" about reasons for major organisational changes, but that figure falls to 53% for middle managers and 40% for front-line supervisors.

Many studies have blamed a lack of 'rolled-up-sleeves CEO involvement' or a lack of managers role-modelling or failing to 'walk the talk'. This puts all the power in the system in the hands of the leaders. Even if an organisation is 'top heavy', this means responsibility for the change lies in the top 10%. Leaving the bottom 90% disempowered and side-lined. This is evidence that traditional top-down change management is not having the desired impact.

Let's leverage the energy of the bottom 90% in order to deliver successful change, not 'fix' our Change Leaders!

Many Change Leaders would say that not all their people are equipped and interested in participating in change. They tell me that their people are change resistant. I don't believe that is the case.

Research shows that most employees have three or more of the required skills needed to participate successfully in a change initiative. They can initiate, think strategically, come up with creative solutions, absorb and understand information about why and how the organisation needs to change and are able to be supportive to others going through change. The same research shows that 75% of employees surveyed were ready, willing and able to make the changes needed to support organisational change. They brought the requisite

community@thechangemakergroup.com

skills including thinking strategically, being solutions focused, having learning ability and being collaborative.

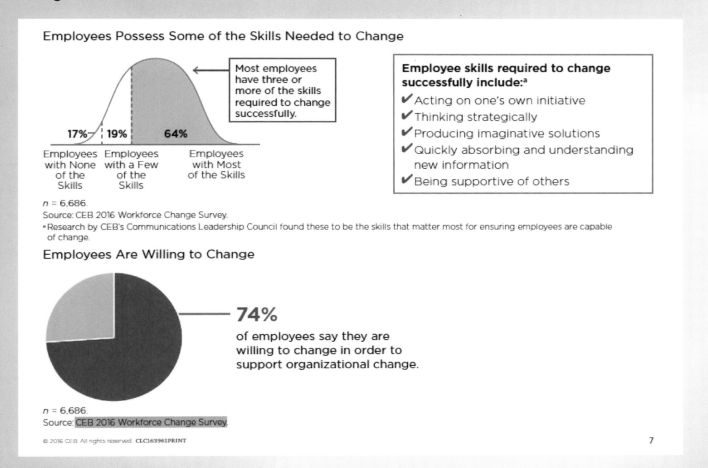

Change and Communication ROI Survey. WillisTowersWatson. 2013 CEB 2016 Workforce Change Survey.

And another piece of research, *The DNA Of A Game-Changer*[7] study by Dr John Mervyn-Smith and Professor Adrian Furnham, shows that organisations are filled with individuals with change capabilities.

Every person inside an organisation can contribute to change by playing one of five roles.

The Game Changer – Transforms the future.

Game Changers see possibilities. They see ways of doing things that others don't. They have a way to imagine how things could be and when they become obsessed with an idea, how things should be. Their potential contribution to an organisation is that radical rather than incremental change.

The Strategist – Maps the future.

Strategists use their business acumen and analytical skills to convert ideas into commercially focused strategies.

The Implementer – Builds the future.

Implementers get things done, they deliver. Their philosophy and practice is one of practical and pragmatic problem solving.

The Polisher – Creates a future to be proud of.

Polishers set the standard for excellence within their role and organisation. They adopt products, processes and procedures with patience for incremental change, and constantly seek to improve.

The Play Maker – Orchestrates the future by getting the best from those around them.

Play Makers focus on the strengths of relationships and by building teamwork.

This model for identifying individual proclivities is known as The GC Index®. This is the first digital assessment instrument to identify Game Changers and the game-changing contributions everyone can make. We have worked with Dr Mervyn-Smith to create *The Change Maker Profile* (powered by The GC Index), to help organisations create Change Making teams. The illustration above demonstrates how the five areas of impact work together holistically to deliver game-changing transformation.

Inside organisations, the research shows that typically only 5% of the population are Game Changers – those people who are coming up with the transformational change solutions. But if we are talking about building self-organising change communities, it's important for every member to have a role to play. Traditional change management fails to tap into the strengths of the community. Typically, the roles of Strategist and Play Maker are assigned to top Leaders. Staff are left to Implement and Polish. But if your contribution is better made at the Strategy formulation stage or as part of the Communications and Engagement workstream, that is where and when you should contribute!

One client that I work with ensures that Game Changers can use their unique strengths to see new and diverse ways of doing things. They 'crowd source' internally and invite Game

Changers to participate. External *crowdsourcing* utilises an unknown crowd to solve a problem or to gather innovative ideas. This crowd may be selected in advance (cathedral) or may be made of every web user (bazaar). This is the practice we generally refer to while talking about crowdsourcing. But internal crowdsourcing utilises a crowd of people known to the organisation to problem solve or generate ideas. The process is opened to all staff members. Having everyone answering a challenge, regardless their business division, can help the company come up with both incremental and disruptive innovation.

Another client uses the concept of a Reverse Leadership group to empower staff at lower levels to use their unique strength in converting ideas into strategies. Staff who are individual contributors are invited to join the Leadership Forum (usually only attended by the top 150 Leaders in the firm) and to put on their Strategist hat and to contribute.

When I worked at the BBC Worldwide, we invited a group of pragmatic problem solvers to join a team we called BRIT (Balanced Regionalisation Implementation Team). This gave the opportunity to implement an important change initiative to a wider population than usual.

Leaders need to create an environment where everyone can contribute to change based on their strengths. It is one of the vital behavioural shifts that is must happen in order for an organisation to adopt doing Change in an Emergent way.

Summary: We Need to Think About and DO Change Differently

The business case for using new change tools and novel approaches is clear. In today's world, the structure, content, and process of work have changed. Organisations must find ways to be more competitive, agile, and customer focused. We can no longer depend on traditional change tools and approaches.

While John Kotter's bestseller *Leading Change*, "is considered by many to be the seminal work in the field of change management", it was written in 1966. New books like *Switch: How to Change Things When Change Is Hard*, written by Chip and Dan Heath must become our 'go to' change manuals.

Outdated knowledge about how people react to change – 'fight or flight' – must be replaced with new knowledge about our brain's elasticity and capacity for 'tend and befriend'. Our knowledge of behavioural psychology and the lessons we have learned from brain science needs to be used more extensively.

And traditional organisational designs that manage change from the top down, using detailed project plans and lots of Programme Managers need to be set aside. Concepts like

Lean, Scrum, Agile, and Holacracy need to be adapted to ensure that all the wisdom inside a firm is being used to initiate and implement change.

In Summary, Emergent Change is needed urgently!

---

[1] Switch: How to Change Things When Change Is Hard. Chip and Dan Heath. Random House. January 2, 2007.

[2] The Difference: How the Power of Diversity Creates Better Groups, Firms, Schools, and Societies. Scott E. Page. Princeton University Press. 2007

[3] The 4 Things Successful Change Leaders Do. Douglas A. Ready. Harvard Business Review. January 28, 2016.

[4] Leading Change. John P. Kotter. Harvard Business Review. March-April 1995

[5] The Prosci ADKAR Model is a goal-oriented change management model to guide individual and organisational change. Created by Prosci founder Jeff Hiatt, ADKAR is an acronym that represents the five outcomes an individual must achieve for change to be successful: awareness, desire, knowledge, ability, reinforcement®.

[6] Build a change platform, not a Change Program" from Mckinsey.com. October 2014 | by Gary Hamel and Michele Zanini

[7] The DNA of a Game Changer Report. Published by eg1. 2015

Michelle Brailsford is known for her passion for building 21st century workplaces: purpose before profit; conversations, not KPI's Trust over Control; performance, not presenteeism. She owns a house in Le Marche, Italy where she enjoys discovering new wine varietals, eating the delicious food, watching brilliant sunsets and swimming in the Adriatic Sea.

TRUST : THE ESSENTIAL LUBRICANT TO ENABLE CHANGE

by Julia Felton

Snapshot: Julia Felton explains why trust is the magic ingredient that can reduce friction and create conditions for enabling high-performance teams that can navigate change. You'll gain an understanding of how powerful trust is and the consequences of a lack of trust in your organisation. Plus, you'll also learn some strategies and tactics you can implement right now to help you build trust within your own organisation.

"Trust is the biggest business commodity of the decade.
Without trust business and relationships falter."

Stephen M. R. Covey

In today's networked and interconnected world, trust has become the new currency – the critical competency for individuals, teams, organisations, and even countries. Trust impacts every situation and relationship, whether personal or professional. Everything of value is built on trust, from financial systems to relationships.

Trust is like water, which is the vital substance that sustains all life on this planet. When there's water, everything flourishes and grows. When it's not there, everything withers and dies. The same is true for trust. Without trust, projects slowly die, team members become dis-engaged and strategies fail. Trust has a lasting impact on your team, and in your organisation. A lack of trust is an organisation's biggest expense and in many cases the principle reason why change initiatives fail.

Trust: The Hidden Business Lubricant

Trust acts like a lubricant. It reduces friction and creates conditions for enabling a high-performance team that can navigate change. How well the team works together is the true indicator of the future success and ability to lead through change. The behaviours that build trust are the same behaviours that help people navigate change, which is why at The Change Maker Group we are passionate about helping companies navigate from the chaos and confusion of change to a culture of collaboration, connection and camaraderie.

Robert A. McDonald, Chairman, President and CEO of Procter & Gamble, when referring to Stephen M. R. Covey's book Smart Trust, states: *"It is both a mindset and a toolbox for 21st-century leadership"*. Trust is an important commodity that cannot be overlooked when building business or initiating change projects. Trust is the glue that holds relationships together. Without trust, there is no harmony in the team or in business, and dis-ease prevails.

The *Fusion Business Blueprint*™ is a great model for navigating change and creating a sustainable business that acknowledges and recognises that it is part of a bigger eco-system and therefore has a social responsibility to adhere to. The three business cornerstones of:

- Expand the leader
- Empower the Team
- Engage the Environment

are aligned together by an Embedded Purpose and effortlessly interact with each other when trust exists to lubricate the interactions. The result is a highly Energised Business Culture that can operate and respond in an agile manner to the changing business outlook.

community@thechangemakergroup.com

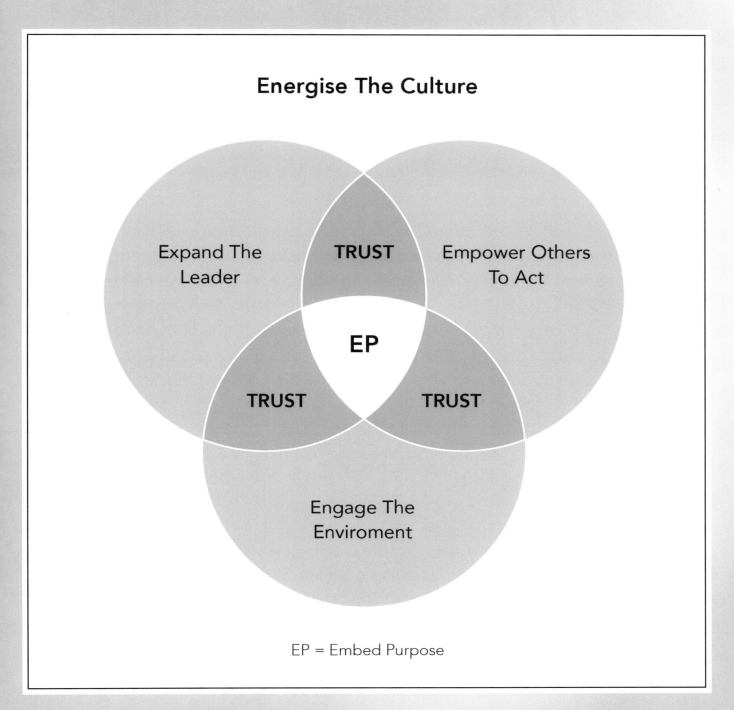

Energise The Culture

Expand The Leader

TRUST

Empower Others To Act

EP

TRUST

TRUST

Engage The Enviroment

EP = Embed Purpose

The Fusion Business Blueprint

What is Trust?

When we speak to clients about trust, whilst everyone understands what it is, many people struggle to explain it. A great analogy to help you articulate and understand what trust is to compare it to money. Each time a leader makes a good leadership decision, trust is built (earn more money). Conversely, each time the leader makes a poor leadership decision, trust is eroded (money lost).

All leaders start with a certain amount of money in their pockets or piggy bank; how they act determines whether that sum of money grows or becomes depleted. If a leader keeps making bad decisions, then eventually the pile of money disappears – they have run out of trust with those they influence. It doesn't matter whether the last blunder is big or small, it will be the straw that breaks the camel's back.

Trust flows from individuals and is the single differentiator of all the greatest leaders. It is rarely talked about as a competency to learn and practice, although this is changing. Trust is no longer a nice-to-have soft skill in business, but rather it is a quantifiable competency that brings dramatic results.

Building trust requires character. It means doing what you say you will do because only when the leader acts consistently in this way will team members be prepared to follow. No trust, no followers, no leadership.

"A one-eighth improvement in leadership trustworthiness resulted in a 2.5% increase in profitability. No other single aspect of manager behavior that we measured had as large an impact on profits."

2002 study by Cornell University

Building Self-Trust

So how does a leader build trust in those that follow them, and in themselves, since good leadership involves leading from the inside out? The answer lies in consistently exemplifying:

- Competence

- Connection

- Character

Ralph Waldo Emerson states that *"Self trust is the first secret to success"*, because just as you can't lead others until you can lead yourself, you can't trust others until you can trust yourself.

In his book *The Speed of Trust*, Stephen M. R. Covey describes the first wave of trust as self-trust. It is all about being credible and developing integrity, intent, capabilities and results that make you believable, both to yourself and others.

Building trust with yourself starts with the small things in life: doing what you say you will do. Paul Dunn of B1G1 calls this *The Power of Small*. For example, being on time to meet friends, not finding excuses for cancelling just because you don't feel up to it, putting personal appointments in your diary and then making sure you keep them (e.g. going to the gym).

I know from my own experience how difficult it can sometimes be to keep those appointments with myself. It is so easy when the alarm goes off in the morning to find an excuse for not exercising today, or not getting up and writing my book. Over these last few months, it has taken courage and determination for me to set aside time to write. Sure, there is always something else pressing to do, but I know that every time I fail to keep these commitments to myself, I feel my self-esteem and self-confidence slipping away and I fail to inspire others to believe in me. They lose trust in me and the net result is that my business suffers.

We all know it intuitively, and research also confirms, that a person's self-confidence affects their performance. This is why Jack Welch of GE always felt so strongly that *"Building self confidence in others is a huge part of leadership."* Furthermore, a lack of self-trust also limits our ability to trust others. In the words of Cardinal de Retz, *"A man who doesn't trust himself can never really trust anyone else."*

It is the small things that a leader does that ultimately impact how people trust them. Often leaders might not realise it, but telling a white lie here and failing to keep an appointment there all impact their credibility. And if they are not credible, then they are not trustworthy; people simply don't believe that the leader will follow through on their actions. Leaders lack integrity when they fail to keep their own standards, and when they fail to live up to their own standards, their colleagues see no reason to either.

The Consequences of Lack of Trust

Trust needs to be reciprocal and shared. We don't trust rules, we trust people. Courage comes from leaders whose responsibility it is to protect the people working below them. People have confidence to do the right thing when they feel trusted by their leaders. It is leaders who energise the business culture to enable team members to reach their full potential, resulting in superior business performance.

Leaders cannot break trust with people and continue to influence them; it simply does not happen. Once trust is lost and the leaders influence is destroyed then team performance dwindles. Once this occurs sales are impacted as people buy from people they know, like and trust. Without trust, the organisation loses productivity, relationships, talent, customer loyalty, creativity, morale, revenue and results. This is why trust, not money, is the currency of business.

"Trust is like a mirror ... once its BROKEN you can never look at it the same again..."
Unknown

Lack of trust is prevalent in business today. Team members no longer trust employers to look after them. Long gone are the days when people had a job for life. Today businesses quickly downsize when economic conditions get tough. There is little loyalty from team members to employers or vice versa. The financial crisis of 2008/9 has made more and more people distrustful of banking institutions, as well as the government's ability to handle these situations.

The diagram below clearly illustrates the consequences and impact of high versus low trust in a business

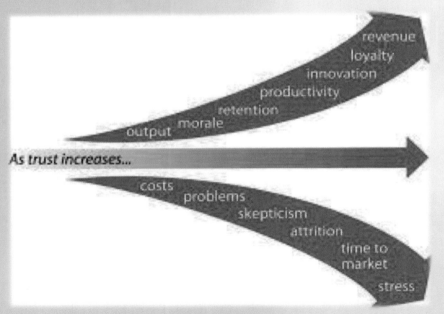

To earn the trust of their team members, leaders must first care for their well-being and connect with them.

To earn trust, trust must be extended. The best way to do this is to create a caring environment that enables people to fully engage their heads and hearts.

High Trust Environments Are Life Changing

In the VUCA world in which we now live there is only one certainty and that is change. Change is forged through relationships and the foundation of effective relationships is trust. During change trust will be tested at best and broken at worst which is why high trust relationships are essential to your change effort's success. When the people you work with trust one another, you have one another's backs as change unfolds. Instead of keeping your head down, you keep an eye on where you can step in and offer extra support. Instead of allowing change to unravel your relationships, you leverage change to strengthen your relationships.

The result is that everyone pulls together in the same direction and no-one is left behind. Communication and engagement improve as team members start asking how they can best contribute and support the change. How can they make a real difference? When the leader and team members are aligned in the right place, contributing to the right work with the right people then team members feel valued and become more highly engaged. Which only has positive benefits for the organisation as productivity and profitability increase.

"Increasing employee engagement by 10% can increase profits by US$2,400 per employee per year"

Accenture

Honest Intentions Create Trust

A high-performance culture can only occur when team members know that the leader's intentions are honest. Being open is perhaps the most powerful way that a leader can create trust. When a leader opens up and has honest conversations, people tend to be more open in return and a genuine interest and respect can develop. Conversely, if the leader is a "closed book", people find it difficult to connect with them; there is no commonality of purpose. This is the reason why open-plan offices have become more popular in recent years. The lack of closed doors makes managers and team leaders more accessible and some of the physical barriers to communication are broken down.

Leaders are also more likely to instil trust in their team members if they demonstrate fairness, especially when making contentious decisions, and if they can admit to their own Achilles' heel and seek to address this. Ultimately though, trust is developed through serving others (and/or a higher cause) as opposed to serving self. Building trust in your abilities is achieved through exuding appropriate optimism and confidence and ensuring that your accomplishments are recognised appropriately.

Breaking the Rules

Trust is the biological reaction to the belief that someone has our well-being at heart – that they care about us. Great leaders are trusted by others to obey the rules. They are also trusted because they are flexible and know when to break them. The rules are there for normal operation. When a situation dictates it, we want team members to break the rules and go the extra mile for customers. This is how great customer service results.

In *Entrepreneur Magazine*, Richard Branson shares the story of when one of his team members did exactly this. They broke the rules to provide exemplary customer service. The essence of the story was that a passenger was flying from New York to London in Virgin's Upper Class and, as a result, was entitled to a complimentary limo pick-up to take them to the airport. For whatever reason, the limo didn't arrive and the passenger was forced to make their own way to the airport.

When the passenger arrived at the airport, they informed the check-in attendant of their experience, and, from her own pocket, the check-in attendant refunded the passenger the cost of his taxi fare to the airport. When the check-in attendant sought to reclaim the money from her superior, her request was declined because she did not have a receipt.

Eventually this story reached the Virgin head office and the check- in attendant was immediately refunded the money and praised for her initiative, which had created great customer loyalty. Conversely, the check-in attendant's supervisor was reprimanded for blindly following the rules without recognising that this was a case where breaking the rules was acceptable because of the customer loyalty that resulted.

The Eight Pillars of Trust

So how do we build trust in organisations? What actions can leaders take to create a trust based culture where team members feel fulfilled and give of their best of each and everyday?

In the book the *Trust Edge*, eight pillars of trust are identified that when used together help individuals and therefore organisations to become more trustworthy. These are:

1. **Clarity**
   People trust the clear and mistrust the ambiguous. Clarity unifies and motivates, it increases morale and inspires trust. Clear communication leads to trusted colleagues, happy team members and satisfied customers.

community@thechangemakergroup.com

2. **Compassion**

People put faith in those that care beyond themselves. Caring leads to trust. Great leaders think beyond themselves and put people before things to improve relationships.

3. **Character**

People notice those who do what is right over what is easy. Building integrity takes work but also yields the biggest rewards. Great leaders always ask: "*Is this the right thing?*"

4. **Competency**

People have confidence in leaders who stay up-to-date with relevant new ideas and concepts. As a leader make sure to continually stretch your mind to discover new ideas, fresh thoughts and concepts. Engage in continual learning and surround yourself with inspiring and motivating people who challenge you

5. **Commitment**

Passion is the essential ingredient of commitment. When people are committed to a cause they will go out of their way to make things happen. People who stick with you when times are tough are those that you can trust.

6. **Connection**

People want to follow, buy from and be around people they like and trust. As a leader ensure you engage and collaborate with team members and customers and really listen to what they need.

7. **Contribution**

People respond to results. Give your attention, resources, time, opportunity and talent to make a difference. As a leader you must deliver results in order to be credible and be trusted.

8. **Consistency**

People love to see the little things done consistently. It gives them security and comfort. Trust is built over time so ensure the same quality of results is delivered every time to build trust.

When these eight pillars are implemented in organisations then leaders enjoy improved relationships, reputation, retention, revenue and results. Which of these trust pillars will you start implementing in your organisation today? What will be the impact on your ability to navigate change if you increase trust levels by just a few percentage points.

From our experience at The Change Maker Group the most highly trusted organisations thrive as they enjoy higher levels of team engagement, morale, productivity and innovation, all factors which enable the business to be agile and respond on-the-hoof to changing business situations.

Julia Felton loves to navigate change whether it be leading teams through cultural change (as she did during the Andersen Deloitte integration) or guiding clients through experiential retreats in nature. Her work encourages clients to challenge the status quo and step out of their comfort zone to experience life from a different perspective. A secret cowgirl at heart, Julia lives in Yorkshire with her herd of four rescue horses. She is an award winning author and international speaker.

CHANGE MANAGEMENT

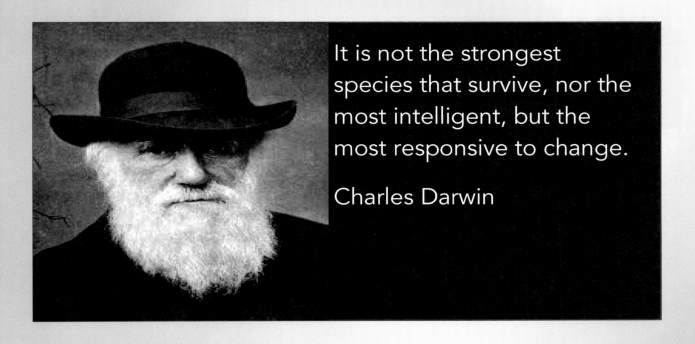

It is not the strongest species that survive, nor the most intelligent, but the most responsive to change.

Charles Darwin

Change won't wait. Change Makers show how to survive and thrive in a changing world.

STAKEHOLDER ENGAGEMENT REVISITED

by Simon Phillips

Snapshot: In this chapter Simon Phillips gives a view of how and why people react differently to change, and reflects on some of the traditional and modern approaches to supporting and managing stakeholders. He also expounds the opportunities that networking provides to support your change.

"Organisations as we know them are the people in them; if the people do not change, there is no organisational change. Changes in hierarchy, technology, communication networks, and so forth are effective only to the degree that these structural changes are associated with changes in the psychology of employees."

Schneider, Breif and Guzzo (1996)

All change is about people and so creating a people strategy for your change programme is a wise first step. Your people strategy is all about how you will engage the Stakeholders. A Stakeholder is simply someone who is either involved in, or impacted by, the project you are leading. No need to dress it up as anything more than that. The common denominator of every successful change programme is the degree to which those involved felt responsible and those impacted felt engaged. The Stakeholders will almost certainly include colleagues, suppliers and customers and may extend out to interest groups, lobbyists and, sometimes, the public (in the form of critics and fans.)

As someone who has trained and coached project managers in the skill of stakeholder management and also written a book all about Networking[1], I have observed a number of overlaps in both the theory and implementation which I think could be advantageously applied to both.

To kick-off, here are three principles common to both activities;

1. Don't wait until it's dry to dig your well

One of the biggest mistakes you can make when it comes to networking professionally is to wait until you need something before starting. Networking is an activity based on the notion of reciprocation. Essentially, you should give, give and give again before you ask. Indeed, in general, you should give with no thought of what you will receive in return. Networking is an every day task. You should seek to expand your network daily to reflect the ebb and flow of relationships. As the lives of people in your network change, they will move away and may become less connected, so constantly adding new connections ensures you can maintain a robust network, ready to spring into action whenever you need it. One such time could be when you have been asked to lead all or part of a new project or initiative. You can ensure your project gets off to a flying start if you have already developed well-formed relationships with the individuals who are identified as key stakeholders.

It follows, therefore, that someone who spends time building and nurturing relationships (i.e. networking) will find it easier to identify and engage the appropriate stakeholders for their projects. Which brings me to the second common principle;

2. For best returns, invest time in people

Time spent connecting, engaging, collaborating, building trust and supporting people in our networks is time-consuming, yes, but it can deliver big rewards and often from the most unexpected sources. The power of weak links in networking terms is a phenomenon highlighting the importance of maintaining links broadly. Often the people who can help us most are not very well known to us. Instead, we may have only met the person who is going to make a game-changing impact on our goals once or twice. However, if we have built a good reputation within our networks, founded on trust and reliability, requests for assistance are answered readily. So it is with developing a reputation amongst our potential stakeholders. Many of your closest stakeholders will be firm advocates and active promoters if you have built a reputation based on integrity and trust.

3. Apply the caring principle

It is a truism in life that people don't care how much you know until they know how much you care. Applying this principle seems quite intuitive when it relates to networking, we respond extremely positively to requests from our greatest supporters. Sales theory would have you believe this is through a sense of obligation, but often it's more of a desire than a chore.

In our change projects, the application of this principle is just as powerful. If the interests of our stakeholders inform and drive our actions, then they too will respond well to our requests for their support. Our desire to deliver improvement or benefit for our stakeholders needs to be both authentic and transparent. If your project does not deliver benefit for all stakeholders, you should still aim to explain *why* the change is necessary or even desirable.

What type of Stakeholder are you dealing with?

Very few lists of stakeholders are homogeneous. What one stakeholder wants or needs can be very different from the next. Consequently, an approach to stakeholder engagement that is not differentiated will not deliver your desired outcomes. Blanket statements and generic messages will join the rest of the white noise your stakeholders encounter almost every minute of the day. If you wish to truly engage your stakeholders, you need to see them as individuals and that's where your challenges begin!

The differences between the individuals in your stakeholder list can be vast. Some will respond well to highly-detailed reports while others will glaze over or simply lose the report in the large pile of unread material covering their desk or clogging up their Inbox. At The Change Maker Group, we use a tool called Clarity4D, based on Jung's theories of preferences, to develop engagement strategies that generate higher levels of buy-in and limit the possibility of resistance.

Edgar Schien has stated; "People don't resist change, they resist being changed."

The quickest way to help someone feel you are not trying to change them is to talk to them in a way that recognises their own preferences. In Clarity4D, those preferences are classified according to four colours.

People who have a **RED** preference want to get to the bottom line of your change proposal, so engaging them is best done through answering the questions in their mind – the Who, What, When, Where, How and Why? Get these across quickly and with enthusiasm and you are well on your way to enrolling an advocate with lots of energy.

Your stakeholders with a YELLOW preference will enjoy understanding the big picture. They love feeling part of a mission and typically they embrace change readily. Talk in pictures and elaborate with stories to really engage them and if you have a few visuals to share too, all the better!

Stakeholders with a strong **GREEN** preference will want to feel that what you are proposing has been thought through with everyone in mind. They do not expect everyone to benefit from the change, but if people are going to be negatively impacted, they will want to be assured that the solution is fair. Due to their friendly nature, these stakeholders will be great at recruiting additional people to the cause once they've committed fully themselves.

Finally, there are those with a **BLUE** preference. Like the stakeholders with a red preference, they will have a number of questions in their head, they just may not ask them all straight-away. Give them time and space to process and review your proposals; this will be easier if you have supplied a comprehensive, written document. For your blue preference stakeholders, facts are critical, so beware of embellishment!

Another tool we use to help us understand the individual needs of our stakeholders is our Change Maker Profile (powered by The GC Index). This organisational diagnostic, provides another useful perspective on the way people like to approach the challenges they face and can help you organise your thoughts as you structure your stakeholder engagement plan.

The five types of people classified by the Change Maker Profile are discussed elsewhere in this book, but if we apply the stakeholder lens, this is what we find;

Strategists like to understand and discuss the big picture and will see how your project fits (or doesn't) with everything else that is happening.

Implementers focus on the work and will be great at helping you understand the scope and complexity of your proposals.

Polishers are fixated on delivering quality outcomes and can provide a healthy perspective on the risks associated with your proposals.

Game Changers provide energy and ideas at every stage of the process. Their free-thinking approach can help when the way ahead is unclear.

Play Makers can review your stakeholders and identify the skills, capability and expertise you need to deliver your proposals.

Typically, your network (and your stakeholders) will be filled with a real mixture of individuals and few, if any, will fit perfectly into any of the four colour energies or five proclivities explained above. Each will instead be a unique blend – a complex and ever-changing, individual with diverse needs and desires. However, the potential to improve your relationships with your stakeholders through "speaking their language" is invaluable.

Next level Stakeholder Mapping

Many of you will be familiar with the standard approaches to stakeholder mapping, starting with the recognition of how close the stakeholders are to the key players in the project team in terms of relationship quality.

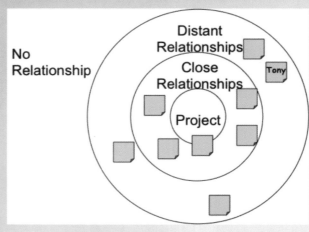

From there, we usually spend time determining whether those same stakeholders have a positive or negative perception of the project and the level of power they have to influence others.

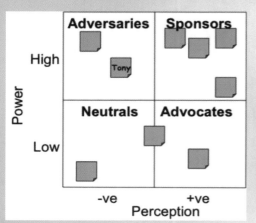

As you can see from this diagram, this thinking process can help us classify the stakeholders into four groups; Sponsors, Advocates, Neutrals and Adversaries. Of course at this stage, we may not be certain how the stakeholders perceive the project but I will come back to that later. For now, as long as we document the assumptions we can keep moving forward. Although, if we stick to this level of stakeholder mapping, we may feel like it has been little more than an academic exercise. We need to add an extra level of thinking to develop the insights more deeply.

The burning question most people want to know about their stakeholders is what level of commitment do they have to helping you? Someone may be influential and they may perceive your project well, but if they are not committed to the outcomes, their support may be half-hearted or, even worse, non-existent. The additional two-by-two matrix below can help.

Determining an individual's likely commitment to something often revolves around their thoughts on what's in it for them? Do they have something to gain or will they be a loser if your proposals succeed? Interestingly, the thing they may be losing may not be substantial; it could simply be their fondness of, or familiarity with, the status quo. What we can be sure of though is the impact their opposition could have if left unattended. We need a plan.

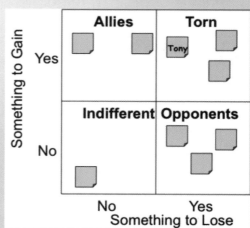

As the diagram above indicates, this classification results in four new types of stakeholders, Allies, Opponents, the Indifferent and the Torn and this last group is potentially the most interesting. Quite often, people err towards the path of least resistance and so, if they are feeling Torn, our job is to listen to their concerns and help them focus on the benefits without them feeling like we are coercing them overtly.

This extra dimension can transform your thinking. Look at Tony in our maps. Initially, we may recognise the distant relationship, observe the power and influence he has and perceive his opposition as insurmountable. However, the additional intelligence reveals Tony has something to gain from the project and suddenly, we have something we can work with; there is a glimmer of hope.

All of which brings us to an important principle of stakeholder management – it requires time and energy.

Stakeholder engagement requires some leg-work

Very few projects are derailed because there was insufficient thinking about the technical solution, or because the project plan was developed using the wrong software. Most projects fail to achieve their original objectives because the stakeholders were not engaged effectively.

As a rule of thumb, stakeholder management is an activity that requires less effort over time and therefore requires a lot of effort up front. Recently, I worked alongside a senior executive as they sought sponsors, advocates and allies for their new leadership development programme. The decision making body contained nearly twenty people and he arranged face-to-face meetings with all of them to ascertain how his proposition could be seen as beneficial to them or for their part of the organisation. By the time he made his presentation to the board, he knew it was going to succeed because he knew exactly how to pitch it to meet the needs of everyone in the room.

Thereafter, only the sponsor had a close interest in the programme and the others were happy with an infrequent update on how well "their" programme was going.

Some may feel that this is a lot of effort, and they would be right. However, from experience, I would suggest that the amount of time it takes to overcome real opposition from a powerful adversary is far greater, especially if they have succeeded in persuading the Indifferent and the Torn that there are considerable problems and issues contained within your proposition.

A tempting approach to engaging all stakeholders at once is to bring them together for a group presentation. This can be effective if you have a unified group in favour of the proposal but this is seldom the case. Let's have another look at the final stakeholder map and view them as a whole group. Bringing everyone together could spell absolute disaster if you haven't put in the leg-work.

The number of Opponents is equal to the number of people who are Torn and your Allies are

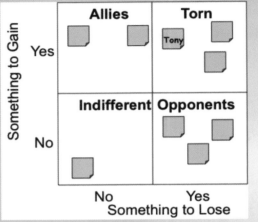

few. It would only take some focused vocal dissent from amongst the opponents and the Torn may suddenly have joined a group that is actively influencing your Allies against your programme. Better to meet everyone with something to lose personally, listen closely and redesign your thinking if it will ensure you can keep your Allies in place and bring the Torn individuals on-board.

The reality is, you build your networks one person at a time and you engage your stakeholders successfully one at a time too. So, what else can we learn from the best networkers?

Good networking habits for Stakeholders

I interviewed almost fifty of the UK's and some of the world's most prolific networkers as research for my book and was constantly surprised at how much of what they said could be utilised in stakeholder management. In no particular order, here are some of the most important habits that Change Makers can learn from effective networkers.

Planning is critical

The best networkers know who will be at an event or meeting, what they will say to them and what outcomes they may wish to achieve. This may be nothing more significant than renewing a friendship but it will be done purposefully. This leaves less to chance and more space for unexpected opportunities to be explored. Similarly, having an explicit stakeholder plan facilitates great outcomes from those chance meetings in the corridor.

Keep in Touch

In networking theory, individuals are nodes in the network and the way to keep the network vibrant is to touch the nodes frequently. "Keeping in touch" is the networkers number one strategy, whether it be virtually or in person. The stakeholder manager needs to be equally conscientious in maintaining their relationships. Updates, both broadcast and in person, are often the difference between a project being viewed as successful or not

See synergies

Networkers see many synergies. How their work fits with the work of a new contact. How their new contact could benefit from talking to specific people in the network and how everyone could benefit from working together to tackle a particular issue. As someone charged with delivering a specific project, it can pay huge dividends to keep an open mind as you engage your stakeholders. Sometimes, an objection can transform into a new opportunity and a major obstacle can reveal a completely different way to achieve the desired outcomes with less effort and expense.

Connect people

The most valuable people in a network are the Connectors. These are the people that make everyone's life easier and provide two people with a new opportunity. Often, the opportunity is in saved time, energy or resources. For the stakeholder manager, connecting stakeholders is a favour that is seldom forgotten and can reap immediate rewards if the connection pairs an advocate of your project with someone who needs additional persuasion.

Follow Up

The activity that marks the difference between the amateur and professional networker is following up. The simple action of keeping a small commitment such as sending some promised information or making a connection cements the networker's credibility. Similarly, engaging stakeholders is an active sport. Planning, meeting, listening, discussing, exploring new options, developing ideas, making connections, summarising…and following up! The last step is the one that ensures all of the previous activities are not wasted.

Getting started

So, when is the best time to get started with your stakeholder management? The best time to start was yesterday and the next best time is immediately. Networking is a lifetime activity and, as intimated earlier, constantly developing relationships can make many of life's activities easier. One of those activities may be your next project…it's time to fall in love with networking

[1] The Complete Guide to Professional Networking, Simon Phillips (Kogan Page)

Simon Phillips is the proud Founder of The Change Maker Group and loves helping individuals manage the turmoil and opportunities in their lives. He started his career in the Change Management division at Accenture and has consulted, trained and coached individuals at all levels inside organisations to make change happen. He is an award winning author and speaker on the topics of personal effectiveness, networking and change and is currently building an App to help identify what motivates and demotivates people. When he is not watching his beloved Wales play rugby he is eating rhubarb!

community@thechangemakergroup.com

THE HUMAN TOUCH : COMMUNICATING SO PEOPLE WANT TO CHANGE

by Karen Dempster

> Snapshot: Getting change communication right can be tricky. Karen Dempster shows how you can get it right by being clear on what the future world looks like, understanding audiences, listening to their ideas and needs and developing communication with them in mind. This will enable change leaders and their organisations to reap benefits.

According to senior leaders, the main reason change fails is a lack of communication[1]. This is hardly surprising, as change should not be about forcing in a new system, strategy or initiative. It should be about people and how they can be energised to change their mindsets and behaviours. Change can be scary, especially if people feel it is being done to them and they have no voice or control.

Despite them intellectually understanding this fact, many organisations force in change in the way they've always done it and get the same results. Communication is often the poor relation to process, system and other non-people aspects in the change approach.

The cost of poor change communication

The cost of not taking communication seriously can be catastrophic for an organisation. Poor communication results in many unwanted outcomes including: business benefits not being fully achieved, relationships being damaged, trust being eroded, employees being less effective, strategies being developed that aren't delivered and systems that aren't fit for purpose. This all builds into an ever-increasing change hangover that raises its disruptive resentment and scepticism every time another senior leader announces the next change that is going to be done to employees.

The CEB Inc[2] identified that failure to communicate early enough with employees about organisational change will cause misconduct to increase by 42 percent. This clearly puts a Company's reputation at risk. Lack of communication about change can directly affect the brand and in turn the bottom line and shareholder returns. The CEB highlighted eight company-wide changes or career moments that carry the greatest risk and chances of misconduct: layoffs; organisational restructuring; change in senior leadership; change in job responsibilities; reduction in benefits; change in direct manager; wage freeze; and hiring freeze.

Information is not communication

Facts, such as the above about employees not having enough communication, can result in knee jerk actions such as sending out more emails, intranet announcements and more. By taking a step back and being clear about what is meant by communication versus information is fundamental to where things can go very wrong or very right.

Sending an email asking people to do something is not really the best way to initiate a major change. Sadly, change is initiated in this way too often. The email is information. Communication only results if the right people read, understand and act on it. Something in the message, and the way it is delivered, needs to connect with them at an intellectual and emotional level. People are more likely to act if they feel something when they receive the message, something that energises them into action.

And to make this a little trickier, employees receive huge amounts of information every day from multiple sources. People are developing, subconsciously, skills to quickly choose what they read and don't read. So, the ability to ensure information results in the desired communication becomes more challenging. The right research will enable change leaders to understand their audience and think about how they can communicate in the best ways to reach them.

Simple steps to communicate so you connect with people

To fully understand and communicate well with the people involved and impacted by the change, consider the following steps:

1. Where do you want to be?

What outcome do you want to achieve? How would you describe this to someone who knows nothing about your company? Focus on the why of the change and not just the what. People just need to get it without jargon, acronyms or techno speak.

How will you know when you have achieved successful change?

What will it look and feel like when you get there? What will people be saying?

What percentage of the success could be attributable to good communication?

2. Who is impacted by the change?

There may be an obvious group of people who are clearly impacted by the change.

But also think about the less obvious people. There are others that interact with the people who are impacted. They need to be supported in understanding the change and what it means for them. Consider internal audiences but also customers and suppliers.

3. What opportunities do you have to involve those who are impacted?

Listening can enable you to reap great rewards. The next three steps below (4-6) require you to listen to those people who are impacted by the change to fully understand their realities.

People in your organisation will have great ideas to do things differently, reduce costs and make initiatives work because they experience the pain every day. Their ideas can sometimes be missed when we don't engage with people early enough or choose to rely solely on the input of leaders or external parties. It's not unusual for a team to be cut back and then six months later the organisation realises they need to rehire because they didn't fully understand the value of that team. Talking to employees avoids some of these costly mistakes and might highlight some easy quick wins. Simple things like moving a coffee machine might result in less time away from the desk!

By involving people early on, they'll feel a greater level of control, valued, that you are listening and they are being taken on the change journey with you, not being left behind.

You can involve them in many ways. You could invite those who feel passionately about the change to join a special group. Some organisations can help you to identify the three percent of people who have the reach to 90% of your organisation so you have a super networked change group. Other people may want to be involved through an online discussion forum where they receive early information and are asked for their views. Or you can involve people through giving them the opportunity to ask questions and suggest ideas at a face-to-face meeting with the right leader who motivates and listens masterfully.

You can continue to listen to employees throughout the change using online quick polls and voice of the employee apps. This will enable you to take a regular temperature check and measure progress.

Importantly, if you ask for ideas then ensure you either empower people to take action or do something with those ideas yourself, wherever possible.

4. Where are they now?

The way change has been introduced historically can leave a change 'hangover'. Numerous negative changes result in a toxic environment where a new change is considered negative despite its true intention. Trust is low and leaders are no longer believed.

In addition, you need to recognise the culture of the organisation, its maturity, the strategic direction, manager capability, values and leadership style.

Take time to review and understand your employee survey, quick poll or voice of the employee pulse check information. You can bring these together into a change environment SWOT (strengths, weaknesses, opportunities and threats).

These factors and insights need to be taken into consideration to ensure you communicate in the right way.

5. What are their preferences?

We all have different preferences for how we like to work and communicate. When we communicate change, we can't tailor communication perfectly for every audience but we do need to consider different people's preferences.

For example, some people prefer evidence and facts, others prefer an engaging and uplifting story delivered in an entertaining way, others want to just get to the point and have little patience for detail. Some people are more introverted and prefer the opportunity to consider information and develop their thoughts before being asked for their ideas. Others are happier to be put on the spot and asked for more instant feedback. Some people prefer visual communication, such as images or videos. Others are happy to read information or listen to people speaking.

We need to consider these preferences as part of our preparation to communicate and there are ways to understand these preferences and accommodate them.

We also need to consider their 'social norms' so what do they see others doing and saying around them, as we tend to feel more comfortable following the norm.

6. What will make them feel good about the change?

community@thechangemakergroup.com

Most changes should, ultimately, have a positive impact for an organisation or why would we make them? Clearly, they may be more difficult from an individual level, either due to the direct impact on someone's job or seeing their colleagues leave.

Generally, when we explain the change fully and why it is happening and give people an opportunity to be involved then they can start to feel energised by what is happening.

For example, it could be a new strategy that for the first time focuses on growth. It may be a new system that supports managers in better managing their teams.

7. What will be their concerns?

People naturally put up barriers to change, especially if they've had a previous bad experience. They will focus on what does this mean to me? Will it make my job harder? Will I have a job? Will I need to retrain? Who will help me?

It's important to be aware and understand these concerns. You can find out this information through small focus group discussions with different populations who have similar characteristics. The same discussion where you explain the change and ask them what energises them.

Build a robust communication plan

Once you have listened fully then you have the information to form a robust and effective communication plan including:

- Communication objectives – specific, measurable, achievable, realistic and timely objectives built on the organisation change outcomes that enable you to measure your success or areas for improvement.
- Communication strengths, weaknesses, opportunities and threats – outlining your current situation and context for communicating your change. This will also help to identify potential risks that require mitigating actions against each.
- Stakeholder analysis and management approach - how you'll enable stakeholders to play a confident and active role.
- Audiences – defined based on their role in the organisation and their role in the change, plus what will change for them specifically – what will stop, start and continue.
- Messages – your story should have a short 'elevator pitch' that can be shared in less than 30 seconds as well as a full narrative that becomes the core story that runs through all you say and do.

- Communication activities – what needs to happen for each audience to take them on the change journey from where they are now to where they need to be, recognising their motivations and concerns. Activities could include interactive roadshows, online chats, drop-in clinics, online scavenger hunts, short and interactive webinars, printed materials or videos. Ensure that every activity will deliver value. A few impactful and effective activities that are delivered well are so much better than trying to do too much.
- Budget – outline the costs for your communication activities. These costs may involve venue hire, refreshments, employee apps or supporting software, posters, animations or videos.
- Timeline – a one-page view or your communication action plan. Ensure you know what other changes are happening and when, as well as the busy times for the organisation. Avoid these periods to reduce the resistance to the change.
- Roles and responsibilities – clarity on who is doing what to ensure activities happen and are fully supported by the right people. Ensure you have the right level of resource and expertise to deliver great communication. It's an investment worth making to avoid risks.

Develop genuine leadership belief and support

Certain people in an organisation are able to inspire and motivate people. They just have that natural ability. Some need a little more help and coaching. But even the best people need the right support and information so they can lead a change confidently. This confidence comes from understanding and believing in the change. How do you build this belief consistently across a group of different individuals?

It's critical that you invest time in having face-to-face or at least virtual sessions with leaders and managers so they can hear more about the changes directly from the most senior leaders. If a leader can't make the time to talk to these people in this way then why should anyone believe in it? By sharing the change, helping people to think about what energises them and to discuss how they can overcome concerns, you can move mindsets. People hear their peers supporting the change, feel a shift in their own thinking and feel supported in overcoming the challenges together. They are also able to go back to their teams with evidence that this is possible. They are better able to communicate about the change with energy and integrity.

Senior stakeholders need to know their role in the change and the specific actions they need to take. A general 'please support this' isn't enough. Provide talking points, frequently asked questions about the change and a slide pack to support them in communicating confidently.

Ask for their feedback about what they hear and what else they need to be effective in their role.

The future of change communication

When communicating, organisations need to move with the changing needs of people and take advantage of innovations that will affect their lifestyle. New opportunities in virtual reality, artificial intelligence and robotics are available now.

For example, virtual reality glasses are available at low cost and can be used with smart phones that many organisations provide to their employees today. The immersive experience of virtual reality can help to engage employees in a vision of the future that change will deliver. Such technology can enable people to experience leaders talking directly to them as if they were standing there in person, regardless of location.

Technology will not replace the uniqueness of personal communication. While it will drive changes in how people communicate, human communication will become increasingly important as we move into a world of greater automation.

Summary

Getting change communication right can be tricky if not properly thought through. Being clear on what the future world looks like, understanding audiences, listening to their ideas and needs and developing communication with them in mind will enable change leaders and their organisations to reap the benefits. It is worth spending the time and money to get this right and avoiding the expensive mistakes that too many organisations encounter through poor communication.

[1]Robert Half Management Resources 2016 survey of 300 US senior managers
[2]Communication thought leaders and part of Gartner.

Karen Dempster enables people to achieve great results through innovative and best practice communication, particularly during periods of change. She specialises in translating strategic goals into simple and meaningful communication that connects hearts and minds. Karen is also a professional photographer, a mother of a 10-year-old son and is currently taking her experience of helping people to communicate into schools.

Change Alchemy: Delivering Game-Changing Transformation That Sticks

by John Hackett

> Snapshot: Traditional thinking tells us that improving business processes is the best way to change culture and behaviour. However, the majority of change projects fail to embed improvements in the long term and fail to fundamentally change the day-to-day experience of organisations. John Hackett explains the primary mistake most change interventions make, the human psychology that must be addressed to deliver sustainable change and the approach needed to make it all happen.

"Alchemy: The seemingly magic art of transforming an element from its original state to a better state. "

The pace of change in the business world is increasing on a daily basis. The encroaching factors of globalisation, technological and social change and in recent times, Brexit are forcing all organisations to take transformation very seriously. Indeed, only those organisations who are able to develop game-changing teams and deliver significant transformation will survive and prosper in an environment where established paradigms are being deconstructed with alarming regularity.

And yet, while transformation has become such a commonly used term in the business world that it is almost de rigueur for any organisation to have some sort of "change plan" or "transformation programme", few organisations are genuinely delivering game-changing levels of transformation.

Furthermore, many transformation projects fail to deliver substantial long-term change, especially in the context of the thinking and behavioural paradigms of people within organisations. In short, transformation often fails to truly transform.

community@thechangemakergroup.com

In this chapter, we will explore the primary causes behind the failure of many transformation programmes, reveal the fundamental mistake made in many attempts to deliver change and discuss a better way to deliver game-changing transformation.

Traditional Transformation

Numerous strategies have been deployed over the years in an effort to deliver that seemingly elusive level of profound change within organisations. The bulk of these transformation methodologies have focussed almost exclusively on interventions around process and technology – i.e. the design of the work and the tools used to deliver it. Indeed, in some circles, this mindset is so pervasive that there is a strong and widely-held belief that attempting to intervene on the thinking and behaviour of the people within an organisation – those who actually design and carry out the work, has little impact and is potentially detrimental. The conventional mindset says "make the process flow better and buy better tools and everything will be OK".

Witness the growth of the "Lean Systems Thinking" movement. Ostensibly arising from the pioneering work of Taichi Ohno at Toyota over 50 years ago and heavily influenced by the insight of W. Edwards Deming, this way of looking at organisational change has become so popular that it is almost the default choice for any organisation seriously considering how it might improve the way its work works. And many people within Lean Systems Thinking circles will often quote Deming's 95/5 rule – the idea that 95 percent of performance is attributable to the system and a mere 5 percent to the thinking and behaviour of the people within it.

One can question what Deming actually meant by this statement as well as consider the context in which he made it. And indeed, it is true that the system governs the level of performance within any organisation. But what of the 95/5 rule as commonly understood by those in improvement circles?

Well, to scrutinise this commonly held belief, we must consider what we mean by *the system*.

The system in the context of the management of organisations is a high level view of the *complete* organisation in relation to its environment. It is a means of understanding, analysing and talking about the design and construction of the organisation as an integrated, complex composition of many interconnected elements that need to work together for the whole to function successfully.

What is often suggested is that the *design of the work* within an organisation is the greatest and most influential element within the system and therefore, the primary point of intervention for those wishing to deliver transformational change. And at first glance, of course it is. *How* an organisation does things would appear to have more impact on customer experience and organisational performance than *who* does them.

But is this really true?

The Organisational System

Let's return to that preconception that "the system" governs 95% of performance and the thinking and behavior of the people within the organisation is only responsible for 5%. Can this simplistic statement really be true?

The argument for this preconception begins to fall apart when one applies a logical view of the *reality* of how an organisational system operates, taking into account *all* of its key elements.

The following diagram illustrates the elements of the organisational system and their relationships:

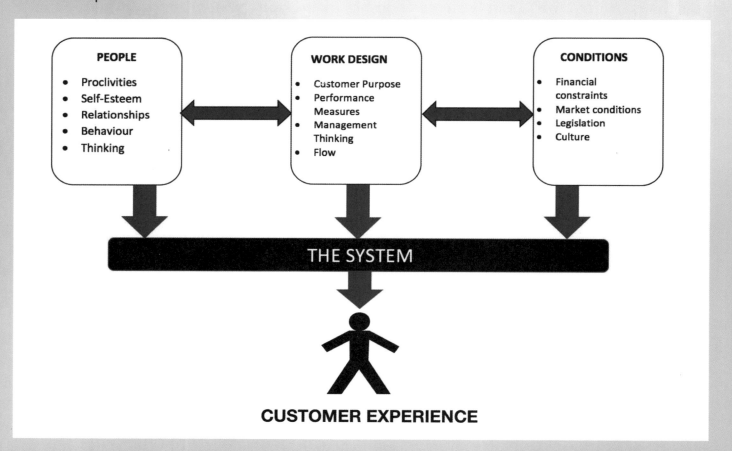

The primary area to consider is the inter-relationships between People, Conditions and the Work Design. As you will see, the contribution, self-esteem, relationships, behaviour and thinking of the People within the organisation influences and is influenced by, the Work Design and the Conditions in which the Organisation operates. This in turn creates the Organisational System.

What this demonstrates is Work Design – the process by which the organisation does things and the means by which customers get what they want – is directly influenced by the multiple facets of both Conditions and most importantly, People. It does not stand alone and it cannot exist outside of People and Conditions. No Work Design can be developed without influence from the Conditions in which it is to operate. But with no People to design and deliver the work, there can be no Work Design.

And it is therefore People who should be the focus of any transformation intervention.

The reason is simple. The profound truth is that the way people think about themselves and the world around them is what, subconciously and conciously, creates the Work Design within an organisation. An individual's beliefs, self-esteem, natural proclivities, relationships and behaviour will have a direct impact on how they manifest their contribution within the workplace. Unavoidably, the design of organisations and the way in which they work is the direct result of the collective thinking and behaviour of the people within them.

To put it in simpler terms – it is People and their influences that decide how an organisation should do things.

The following diagram demonstrates how the response of the individual to the plethora of internal and external influences profoundly affects their assumptions about how work should be designed and delivered.

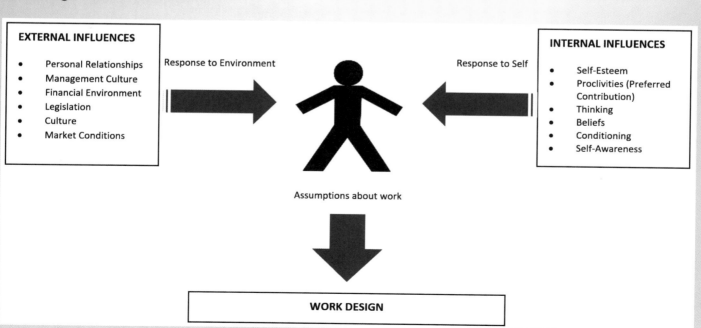

So where does that leave the 95/5 assumption? Well, it is an unavoidable truth that in fact, People ARE the system. Or more accurately, the system is the product of the People in it. The system is created by the People. And it is this fundamental truth that we need to understand if we are to deliver game-changing transformation that sticks.

Why Changing People Makes Transformation Sustainable

As explained earlier, many Transformation initiatives fail to embed within their host organisations. While the causes of this phenomenon may appear elusive, in many cases, these failures follow an observable and predictable pattern, which typically manifests as follows:

- The interventions applied disrupt the existing *work* paradigm, creating a changed perception of how work should be designed and managed amongst the individuals within the organisation.
- The *personal* paradigms of the individuals involved do not *significantly* change, leaving their pre-existing self esteem levels, relationships, assumptions etc. in much the same condition.
- Initially, benefits are seen as a result of the new work paradigm.
- Over time, the work paradigm subtly shifts to become incrementally closer to its original state prior to the intervention.
- After a significant period of time, perhaps a year or more, process, performance and culture have either returned to their original states or deteriorated to a worse condition than was apparent at the start of the intervention.

The cause of this pattern lies with the *personal* paradigms of the individuals concerned. Commonly, Transformation interventions fail to address the thinking and behaviour of the people within an organisation, which results in their personal paradigms being unaltered and therefore, the resulting outcomes continue to manifest themselves in much the same way. This is obscured in the short term by the disruption created by the introduction of a new work paradigm but once the intervention is over and business as usual is reinstated, there is nothing in place to prevent the individuals acting out their paradigms as before. This slowly causes the work paradigm to shift back to that which was most comfortable for the individuals concerned. In short, the failure to change the people means that the process in turn cannot be changed sustainably.

In essence, if one's overall view of the world doesn't change, small adjustments will always revert back to the original baseline. A common example of this is seen in some individuals looking to lose weight and increase their exercise levels. After an initial flurry of activity and

community@thechangemakergroup.com

some early benefits, they slowly revert back to previous habits and the weight lost is regained. Why? Because the individual's core beliefs did not change so the eating / fitness change could not be sustained.

The following chart illustrates how a lack of change in the personal paradigm of individuals within an organisation gradually drags the work paradigm back to the original baseline:

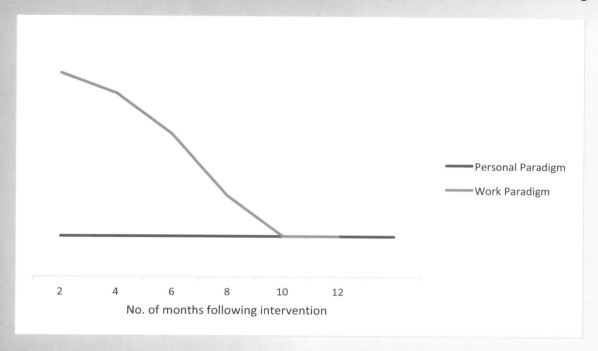

It is clear then, that game-changing transformation cannot be achieved without first developing the thinking and behaviour habits of individuals involved in the design and management of the work. We simply cannot continue to abstract process and technology from the dynamics of people within our organisations if we are to deliver a step-change in the organisational transformation game. To ignore the people element is to condemn any change programme to likely failure.

Game-Changing Transformation Requires Game-Changing Individuals

So how do we harness people in an intelligent way in order to deliver this elusive transformation? Well, as history will readily demonstrate, game-changing shifts have always come from the thinking innovations of individuals. It is the profound leaps in thinking about the design and delivery of products and services which have moved industries forward – it has always been people who have changed the game. A big change in an individual's personal paradigm results in a big change in organisational paradigms.

It turns out that focussing on changing the paradigm for how we design a process or what type of IT system we should buy, the traditional approach to Transformation, prevents the bigger picture from being seen with sufficient clarity. The bigger picture is this – game-changing transformation comes from game-changing individuals. When people are engaged in seeing the world beyond their existing paradigm, change, indeed radical change can be unleashed. When game-changers are engaged and supported, paradigms crumble and transformation flourishes.

It stands to reason that if we can sufficiently modify the paradigms of individuals, then their view of the design and management of work will subsequently alter. If in turn we can demonstrate to them how best to apply their personal strengths to the systemic redesign of their work, they will be equipped with the skills to deliver change going forward. The shift in the personal paradigm creates the shift in the work paradigm. This is the key to unlocking *sustainable* transformation.

If we can release game-changing shifts in paradigm, then we will invariably get game-changing transformation.

Everyone Can Make A Game-Changing Impact

But some may view this proclamation with a healthy dose of scepticism, on the basis that not every individual is a naturally inclined game changer. However, fascinating new research has demonstrated that there may be more game-changers out there than one would at first imagine. The DNA Of A Game-Changer study by Dr John Mervyn-Smith and Professor Adrian Furnham shows that game-changing individuals exist in many organisations, but they are often supressed by internal culture and management practices. What's more, the research also identified that game-changers require support from individuals with complementary skills in order to manifest their impact. A game-changer alone cannot necessarily change the game without the right balance of individuals around them to help implement and refine their vision. This in essence, suggests every individual has a part to play in changing the game. As Nathan Ott, CEO of eg.1 who commissioned the DNA Of A Game-

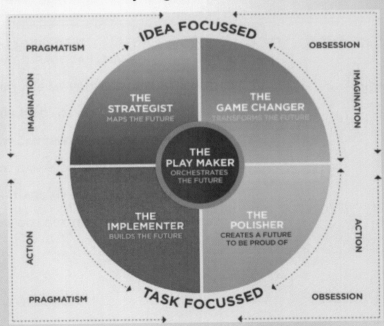

community@thechangemakergroup.com

Changer research says – "not everyone can be a game-changer, but everyone can make a game-changing impact."

What this means in practice is that every individual possesses a natural set of proclivities or impacts which govern the way they personally influence the design and management of work. It is these proclivities that can be identified and developed to shift the individual's personal paradigm, regardless of their natural inclination.

But what are these other impacts? The research identified that there are in fact five key proclivities – the type of impact particular individuals are most inclined to make within the work environment, which can be identified and harnessed in all teams. These are as follows:

The Game Changer – Transforms the future

The Strategist – Maps the future

The Implementer – Builds the future

The Polisher – Creates a future to be proud of

The Play Maker – Orchestrates the future

This model for identifying individual proclivities is known as The GC Index. We have worked with Dr John Mervyn-Smith to create *The Change Maker Profile* (powered by The GC Index), to help organisations create Change Making teams. The following illustration demonstrates how the five areas of impact work together holistically to deliver game-changing transformation.

What the Change Maker Profile shows is simple – a game-changing team is essentially all about having radical ideas, making sense of them, putting them into practice, making them brilliant and ensuring everyone works together to make it happen.

It is about using every individual to their fullest, based on their personal inclination and strengths to change the work paradigm.

This model opens up a tremendous opportunity for game-changing transformation. The message is simple – if we can develop each individual within a team to perform to their maximum impact, a game-changing team can be created.

However, there are additional advantages. Understanding the impact each individual can make clearly has significant benefits in mapping out the recipe for change. And yet there is an even more profound and transformative outcome of identifying an individual's impact in their organisation. It turns out that understanding one's impact and role within a team in the context of creating game-changing transformation delivers an immediate and significant boost to self-esteem.

Why is this important? It's simple – self-esteem is one of the greatest limiters to human performance in the workplace. When an individual feels confident about their professional impact, they are happier and crucially, more productive. They understand where they fit in, how better to interact with colleagues and the tangible outcomes of their own efforts. Conversely, when an individual is unconfident about their abilities, they are less productive, less likely to interact well with colleagues and more risk-averse.

Returning to the internal influencers that affect individuals, it is clear that self-esteem has a profound impact on both the ability of a person to influence the design and management of work and their level of engagement and contribution to the process. Effectively, a group of individuals with poor work-based self-esteem are likely to produce sub-optimal work designs. Without first transforming these individuals' self-esteem, the organisation itself cannot be transformed.

The following illustration shows how work-based self-esteem is formed:

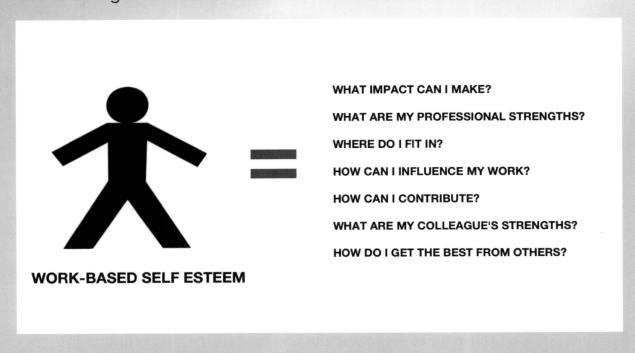

WORK-BASED SELF ESTEEM = WHAT IMPACT CAN I MAKE?

WHAT ARE MY PROFESSIONAL STRENGTHS?

WHERE DO I FIT IN?

HOW CAN I INFLUENCE MY WORK?

HOW CAN I CONTRIBUTE?

WHAT ARE MY COLLEAGUE'S STRENGTHS?

HOW DO I GET THE BEST FROM OTHERS?

community@thechangemakergroup.com

Individuals with poor work-based self-esteem deliver poorer results. Those with strong work-based self-esteem deliver excellent results.

Because work-based self-esteem comes from understanding one's impact in the context of a game-changing team, substantial individual paradigm changes can be unlocked by helping a person to understand and appreciate their natural proclivities and thus boosting their self-esteem.

Change Alchemy: Game-Changing Transformation Through The Potential of People

So understanding the individual impact of each member of a team can help us to improve work-based self-esteem, develop a game-changing approach and make sure everyone is working to their maximum impact.

But how does this deliver game-changing transformation?

Well, you have to take it a stage further. I return to those crucial elements I mentioned earlier – process and technology. As I explained, traditional approaches to transformation focus on improving both of these, usually via one of the many improvement methodologies that are in use throughout the business world. But what is often missed is the opportunity to engage a team in a way which best utilises the natural proclivities of each individual to develop game-changing approaches to the way in which the work is designed and managed.

This is important because all too often, short term improvements to the design of work are made, but individuals receive little significant personal development. As I outlined earlier, the end result is commonly a reversion to type over time. The improvements fail to embed because the individuals within the team have not significantly changed.

However, there is a better way to deliver transformation. And it is called *Change Alchemy*.

Alchemy is the mythical art of taking an element and by applying the appropriate processes to it, transforming it from its original state to a better state. The ancient alchemists believed that each element required its own unique process in order to achieve its transformation – this demanded an appreciation of the exact nature of the element and the relevant levers for change. A well-known example of this idea is the belief that any base metal could be turned into gold so long as the appropriate process for doing so could be identified and implemented.

Change Alchemy is a method for transformation which applies this thinking to the fostering of game-changing teams through the development of the thinking and behaviour of individuals. It uses this as the lever to deliver game-changing transformation.

In practice, the method works as follows - identify the proclivities of the individuals, develop them to play to their personal strengths and then engage them to redesign their work from a systems perspective as a game-changing team.

The beauty of this method is it addresses *all* of the elements of the organisational system – People, Work Design and Conditions. However, it starts with People as the first point of intervention.

It is accomplished with a simple underpinning framework.

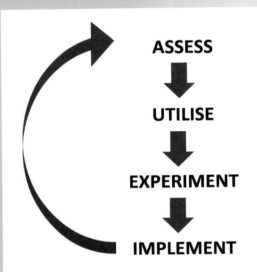

ASSESS

Understand the present condition of people, purpose, process and performance. Identify the proclivities (preferred impact) of the individuals delivering the work through the GC Index Assessment.

UTILISE

Utilise the proclivities of the people to determine innovative ways of meeting purpose within the constraints of the present and future environment. Teach the team how to work to their individual potential to improve the work. Enhance self-esteem by demonstrating the value of each individual's impact in improving the work and meeting the customer purpose.

EXPERIMENT

Encourage the people to carry out experiments in a safe-to-fail environment to determine the best way of meeting customer purpose.

IMPLEMENT

Implement the improved working model and monitor performance. Return to Assess whenever system conditions change.

The Assess, Utilise, Experiment, Implement cycle is the underpinning framework for Change Alchemy. It is designed to facilitate the transformation of a service at a systemic level through a clear and logical approach that both imparts experiential learning and allows for flexibility in the delivery mechanism to suit specific situations. In other words, *Alchemy*.

The logic of the stages in the cycle works as follows:

ASSESS

Provides a clear and holistic understanding of the current circumstances that affect the delivery of the customer purpose, identifying the characteristics of the individuals delivering the work, the means by which it is carried out and the environment in which it is delivered.

Assess asks:

community@thechangemakergroup.com

- What are the proclivities of the individuals delivering the work?
- How do these proclivities make up the impact of the team delivering the work?
- What is the Purpose of the work from the customer's perspective?
- What environmental factors affect our ability to deliver the work?
- How well are we currently delivering the work?
- How can the proclivities we have at our disposal be used to deliver the work in a way that better serves the customer purpose?

To carry out Assess we need to identify:

- People (Proclivities and Behaviours)
- Performance (Purpose, Achievement from Customer's Perspective)
- Work Design (Flow, Value / Waste, Technology)
- Environment (Market, Financial Constraints, Competitors, Legislation)

Delivery mechanisms for Assess include:

- The GC Index Assessment Individual Profiles
- The GC Index Team Profiles
- Coaching and Feedback on The GC Index outcomes
- Purpose / Measures / Method Workshops
- Data Collection and Analysis

UTILISE

Harnesses the proclivities of the team carrying out the work to analyse the body of evidence collected at Assess and determine innovative means of better delivering the purpose from the customer perspective, through redesign of the work. Reinforces self-esteem by focussing individuals according to their strengths to create innovation and demonstrating how their impact contributes to game-changing improvements in meeting customer purpose.

Utilise asks:

- How do we work together as a team, playing to our individual strengths to deliver the best possible solution to achieve our customer's purpose?
- What proclivities do we need to make sure we can deliver what is required and do we have them within our team?
- How do we develop our proclivities to maximise the potential for successfully meeting our purpose?
- What is a better way of designing our work so the customer purpose is achieved?

To carry out Utilise we need to identify:

- How best to ensure each individual is able to develop their proclivities to achieve innovative work designs

Delivery mechanisms for Utilise include:

- Behavioural assessment (focussing on the behaviours required to positively manifest individual impact)
- Brainstorming workshops
- Business Process Review (for larger programmes)
- Identification of measures to test achievement of purpose

EXPERIMENT

Provides the opportunity for the team to test the alternative approaches to delivering the work developed at the Utilise stage. The experiments are carried out in a safe-to-fail environment to ensure maximum engagement and learning opportunities.

Experiment consists of:

- Testing alternative approaches in a safe-to-fail environment and monitoring the outcomes
- Determine the best approach to take forward to ensure maximum achievement of purpose
- Delivery mechanisms for Experiment include:
- Safe-to-fail experiments
- Analysis workshops to consider outcomes

IMPLEMENT

The successful experiments and measures are implemented into the work environment as the new means of operating. The cycle returns to Assess when system conditions change.

Paradigm Alignment

By following the Change Alchemy model, we overcome the limitations of traditional transformation methodologies. The key is the disruption and evolution of the personal paradigms of the individuals within a team and then the application of the new paradigm to the design of the work.

community@thechangemakergroup.com

Because the point of intervention within Change Alchemy is the individuals concerned as opposed to the work design, we create a situation where the work paradigm is pulled towards a healthier personal paradigm instead of being progressively dragged down to its original baseline by an unhealthy personal paradigm.

The following illustration demonstrates how this works:

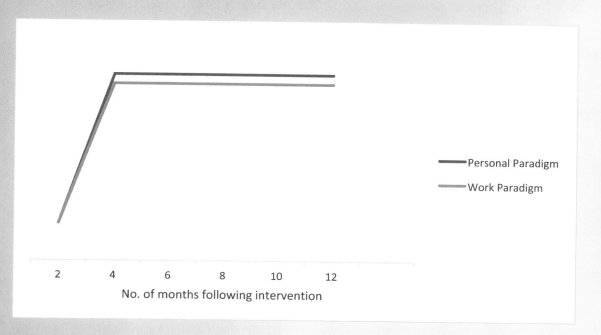

Summary

So an opportunity awaits every organisation. Assess your teams to understand their individual impacts, utilise their skills to deliver innovative ideas for improving the design and management of their work, let them loose in a safe-to-fail environment to try out and refine their ideas before finally, implementing amazing improvements.

You will find that game-changing transformation becomes the norm, rather than the exception.

John Hackett has over 10 years experience in management roles delivering change in processes, business systems and people. He is the founder of the Change Alchemy approach to business transformation and a regular speaker at conferences and events and holds webinar sessions for a large number of professional associations. Outside of work, John is keenly engaged in charitable and community activities such as leading a Resident's Association and is a longstanding member of the Round Table.

The Art of Coping with Complexity: WICKEDD©
solutions in a Wicked VUCA World

by David Walker & Nicky Carew

Snapshot: How do we manage complex problems – not by ignoring them! David Walker and Nicky Carew take a leaf out of the book of science to help make sense what are commonly known as Wicked or VUCA problems and to create a strategy to manage them.

It's in the name, at The Change Maker Group we deal in change. Change is omnipresent, faster, less linear, more democratic and definitely more complicated to manage than it used to be. Communications are immediate and long gone are the days when we just went along with "the authority". Problems become more complex as more influences impact the situation – hence the protracted and often unsuccessful initiatives to tackle global warming, universal healthcare, and things that directly affect our everyday work and family life like work-life balance.

This is particularly true in organisations and businesses. The issues leaders have to deal with are multi-faceted, with many stakeholders and across many boundaries. The 'answer' is seldom clear. Everything you do creates another problem down the line.

Some organisations use the term 'VUCA' - *Volatile*, *Uncertain*, *Complex* and *Ambiguous* problems. In public service, they also know about these complexities – they call them 'wicked' issues. The term reflects the common belief that some issues cannot realistically be solved, but doing nothing isn't an option – global warming would be an extreme example.

There is something special about wicked or VUCA problems – they are not just complicated. Complicated problems are 'tame' problems – difficult in themselves but where a best solution will emerge and a standard operating procedure could be or has been developed (eg: heart surgery, building a bridge, scheduling a football league).

Wicked issues are complex – they are woven into their environment. For example, you could, supposedly, manage the NHS using the logic that medicine and services are provided purely

community@thechangemakergroup.com

on medical need. But that answer is not as straightforward as it may first appear, the population is ageing, obesity is a problem, treatments more complex, drug companies need incentives to create new cures, resources are finite – decisions have to be made but on what criteria? A decision made on social care has an impact on hospital beds; staffing on immigration need. These wicked issues cross all sorts of boundaries and never stay constant.

But something must be done. These problems cannot be left to fester on the basis they are too complex. Unfortunately, the pressure to be seen to act decisively often induces leaders to resolve the problem as if there was a linear cause and effect. One high profile panacea to global warming was investing in biofuels, only it led to the destruction of tropical forest, the one protection we have to reduce carbon dioxide.

Here we outline our thinking about how to work through progressing wicked or VUCA issues.

How, then, do we get a grip on wicked issues?

If you could really understand what makes a wicked issue different then the way to tackle it becomes clearer. A useful analogy is to regard tame issues like physics – once you know the rules (or laws in physics) then an outcome can be predicted with any intervention.

Wicked problems are more like biology – life evolved according to the environment at the time, it continues to adapt and mutate, it has history as have wicked problems. Biology and wicked problems involve complex relationships that cause interactivity that is hard to anticipate. We have taken a leaf from the book of biological science and how they get to understand complexity. Biologists observe, record, tinker and observe more. A true leader in a wicked world learns to manage wicked problems in a similar way – so we developed our *WICKEDD©* solution as a means of helping leaders in a wicked VUCA world!

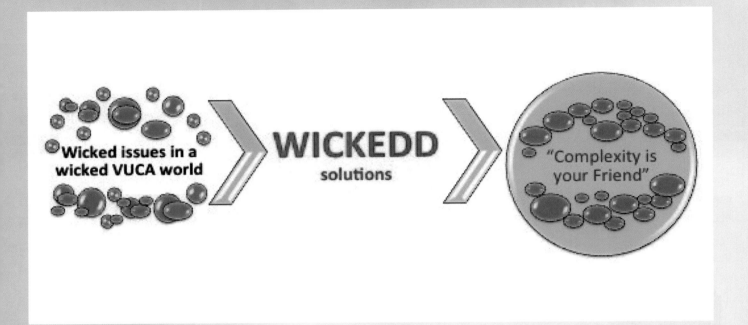

"Wicked issues need WICKEDD© solutions"

Taking our 'leaf' from the biologists – they conduct a field study to understand as much as possible about their subject. Similarly leaders need to take stock before leaping in with a management solution. Wicked issues are really tricky to define, tricky to control and tricky to solve.

So *WICKEDD* is a simple mnemonic for an approach to work through wicked issues. Each aspect of *WICKEDD* can have various techniques and tools applied, but the principal approach to getting control of a tricky issue is the same. If the problem can't realistically be *solved* at least we can move it on to a better outcome and minimise the unforeseen consequences. That way we can help '*complexity be your friend*'.

community@thechangemakergroup.com

"Wicked issues need WICKEDD© solutions"

WHAT, WHY, WHERE taking a helicopter view of the situation with no preconceived solutions.

INTERDEPENDENCIES working out all of the aspects of the wicked issues, getting to grips with the interconnectivity.

CAUSALITY what are the root causes, what is taking us away from the route to our Vision?

KNOWLEDGE what do you know, what don't you know, what do you really need to know?

ENGAGE who needs to be involved to help diagnose how to handle the situation and to create collaboration?

DIAGNOSE now better informed, what is the full current information and where do you need to get to - what is the vision for the solution state?

DO the action points you have identified and monitor impact. What new adaptive outcomes have emerged, what loose frameworks may help make people more adaptive?

Taking each part of the WICKEDD principle:

WHAT, WHY, WHERE – taking a helicopter view of the situation with no preconceived solutions. That especially means not advocating what worked previously because you won't yet know what is influencing this problem at this time. So each wicked issue needs to be seen as novel. What is the effect, why is it happening, where is it having impact? The answers will be new each time. The nature of wicked issues is that they aren't tame and based on a routine or stylised problem-solving process.

INTERDEPENDENCIES – working out all of the aspects of the wicked issues, getting to grips with the interconnectivity. If you change this ... what will happen to that...? The Accident and Emergency performance target resulted in queuing ambulances to ensure the 4 hour target wasn't compromised. For each problem interdependencies can be found in what feeds into the problem, what this problem changes and what stakeholders have an interest in the problem.

CAUSALITY – what are the root causes of this problem? How and when did it appear, what systems encourage it, what behaviours reinforce it? What is taking us away from the route to our Vision? It is well known that correlation is not causality but it is not always clear what is causing what or what is happening to make it seem like it correlates. You can look up the famous correlation of ice cream sales and murders to illustrate this! Biologists have to test their hypotheses and observe what happens to understand how the system works. Leaders might feel the need to quickly pilot a range of solutions before really understanding what will work in moving forwards.

KNOWLEDGE – what do you know, what don't you know, what do you really need to know? Mark Twain said *"It ain't what you don't know that gets you into trouble. It's what you know for sure that ain't so."* This is almost the perfect cause of wicked problems! What do you know about the problem and, as importantly, about the people involved whose behaviour will impact on the wicked issue and ultimately any progress towards a solution. In 2000 an Israeli day-care centre started fining parents who were more than 10 minutes late collecting their children. Intuition would suggest this would deter late parents – but actually the problem rocketed! Before the fine, parents felt bound by a social contract to do their best to collect on time, after the fine they viewed it as a financial transaction and felt no guilt.

ENGAGE – having identified who needs to be involved in diagnosing and improving the situation this can be the most unpredictable and difficult part of the wicked solution. People, that is pretty much all of us, prefer stability to change. They will unconsciously gravitate to solutions that give us fastest relief or a feeling of certainty. However despite that extra chocolate biscuit or glass of wine the problem may not have gone away. To create a successful collaboration of people who will engage in the wicked problem and create a *WICKEDD* solution they in turn need to have collective responsibility. The more diversity you can build into the engaged stakeholders, the more challenging the ideas, the more creative outcomes you will have. This is where successful leadership skills to get full engagement are key.

DIAGNOSE – now better informed, with the best information you can have - what is the vision for the solution state? How are you going to mitigate other potential complications?

community@thechangemakergroup.com

Are there interim states that can be achieved that move us in the right direction? With all parties fully committed and willing to engage as participants what can you agree that will help the solution? The Kyoto protocol in 2005 may not have solved global warming but it was as good as it could have been under the circumstances.

DO – the action points you have identified and, most importantly, monitor impact. What new adaptive outcomes have emerged, what loose frameworks may help make people more adaptive? But hold onto your plans lightly and don't be afraid to do something different if the outcome is not what you expected or the wicked issue mutates or evolves – that is the nature of wicked problems.

Each of the aspects of *WICKEDD* help shape what needs to be done to get to a fully-rounded action plan, and, with agility in execution, get control of a wicked issue.

Ideally of course, in a paper such as this we would be citing excellent examples of solved wicked issues. But the very nature of wicked issues is that so few of them are ever 'solved'. As you reveal one solution another wicked issue pops up. There will always be problems with the Health Service provision but we can make it better. Likewise we are a long way from any agreement that will solve global warming and the best we can hope for is a slowing down - 'falling forward' if you like.

However, one notable wicked problem has been a great success lately after many years of trying – the teenage pregnancy rates so alarmingly high in the 1970s and 80s (55 conceptions per 1000 teenage girls aged 15-17) are now at a level, still high but more akin to our European neighbours of 21 per 1000. While linear solutions were prevalent in the early years (ostracise 'them', deny 'them' support, stop encouraging 'them' with sex education) the level seemed to keep rising with all the social problems that came with it. Results were only achieved when the focus was on cross-agency support, relationship education, easy to use contraceptives and good support for young parents (all things that were previously deemed to encourage the problem).

What is going to get in the way of resolving wicked issues?

The story of the teenage pregnancies illustrates human nature often finds that the ideal way of handling wicked issues challenges our natural way of behaving. So we have identified 8 behaviours that are the Achilles heel for all strategic leaders handling wicked problems.

Beware the temptation to simplify - It is vital to rid yourself from the belief that any single 'logical' solution or linear action plan will tackle a wicked solution or that a single 'expert' can make sense of it. It will result in premature unconstructed solutions and then unforeseen consequences.

Beware short-sightedness - We all have leanings to particular actions or ways of thinking that have worked well for us, but this can lead to focusing on one thing, which prevents you from seeing something else. Wicked issues need tackling from all directions, and watching from every angle to see if the results are as anticipated. That is not to say that actions are not best dealt with quickly – procrastinating will never fix a wicked issue, and agility is key – it is that one narrow action will not solve the issue.

Beware silos - Ever present in most organisations as systems and projects seem to create them. Like other 'biological' constructs they have evolved from a time when they were useful, but silos create insularity and sub-optimal thinking and solutions. They also destroy trust and can create a culture of blame – it's 'them' not 'us' – which feeds the kind of behaviours that lead to wicked issues never moving towards any form of solution. More and more organisations are finding ways to break down these arbitrary barriers – like the Kings Cross bio-tech park where different companies share space where people can meet others to play with ideas and spark creative solutions.

Beware the expert - Can someone really give you the solution to your wicked problem? Wicked issues are rare events – your wicked problem is a new creature that has never been seen before. They are not repeated in any way that a learned response will provide a practical solution. All wicked solutions are judgement calls and there may be many routes to the desired outcome, with interim steps, mini-visions, islands of stability – whatever it is that helps get towards the ultimate vision. You will always have to go through the discipline as described in our WICKEDD approach.

Beware lack of diversity of thought – Success is built on collective intelligence. We tend to feel more comfortable with like-minded people but that will lead to convergent thinking. Different viewpoints, different experiences, different attitudes will challenge thinking, nurture deeper insight, help understand the problem better and create a more compelling strategy to engage all stakeholders. In our internet-supported world, be careful not to try to get a self-researched Google solution to your wicked issue – treat the internet as a source of knowledge, rather than a solution engine as your wicked issue is unique.

Beware your urge to control - Leaders have been rewarded for their decisive behaviour, their certainty and authority. Indeed what will work with wicked problems may even be dangerously viewed as inconsistency, even indecisiveness. It takes great skill and leadership ability to be comfortable with uncertainty (the poet Keats called it negative capability). In a

community@thechangemakergroup.com

wicked VUCA world your issues are unlikely to be solved with a myopically followed 1-year or 5-year plan – again, agility is key.

Beware fear of failure – By now you will have the feeling that wicked problems are impossible to get right. So fear of failure will paralyse you. If there is one thing that wicked problems need, it is to do something that you hope will improve the situation. Sometimes it will not work. You can improve your chance of success by engaging in WICKEDD. Demonstrating traits of flexibility and agility as a collective, monitoring progress and the evolving nature of the wicked issue together means that you are jointly mitigating the risk of failure. If you have nurtured collective responsibility then the failure is not yours alone and you deal with the learnings as a positive for the future.

Beware information overload – It is tempting to get stuck collecting and analysing information and data on these complex issues but the most reliable information comes from observing the results of an intervention, with careful steps and islands of stability. In a wicked VUCA world you will never have perfect information – you just have to work out what you really need to know, find out the information quickly, and start to get control of your wicked issue.

Conclusion

Wicked problems are inherently messy. Each solution may well spur unintended consequences that, in turn, may require more solutions. Uncertainty is the reality. As more and more problems exhibit volatile, uncertain, complex and ambiguous characteristics the new age leaders need to have the ability to see what is good in each different situation. Partial and whole solutions will not be drawn from the rulebook but rather from collective responsibility, experience, reflection and good judgement.

There are masses of techniques and procedures that can be deployed to help you build and monitor an approach to controlling your wicked issues and developing solutions, but key is to move yours and stakeholders thinking towards developing plans that have the inherent flexibility and controls to adapt to an evolving issue.

WICKEDD© will help with that.

David Walker is a programme management and change professional, with a broad background across business sectors and functions. He is also a qualified accountant, but contests that he is not boring. David lives in Northamptonshire with his family, is an avid rugby fan, is heavily involved in his local community, and writes the occasional pantomime.

Nicky Carew has over 30 years' experience of working with senior executives to develop their skills to manage in an increasingly complex environment and has a Masters in Executive Coaching. She lives on the site of 1066 Battle of Hastings and still gets excited by rainbows, watching the International Space Station go overhead and meteor showers.

community@thechangemakergroup.com

HOW WE, AS INDIVIDUALS, DEAL WITH CHANGE

Change can feel like hard work. We know we should be 'agile', open to new ideas but few of us find it easy.

Here our Change Makers identify some of the things that get in the way and offer real down to earth ways to help you deal with your changing world.

BUILD YOUR RESILIENCE FOR WORK AND LIFE IN JUST EIGHT MINUTES A DAY

by Vanda North

> Snapshot: Change can be hard and you need all your energy and resilience to manage it well. Vanda North helps you gain back your 'bounceability' and learn to build your resistance for all life's challenges.

1. Is resilience needed?

What is the one trait that is imperative for delivering success whether as an individual, family, community, company, or even a country? It is resilience! That is the ability to take whatever change is happening and as necessary recover, regroup, learn, plan your next action and rise up again. The good news is that this can be an acquired skill; whatever your temperament you can attain coping strategies which will provide you with both the strength of the oak with the flexibility of the willow. Resilience starts with you and is built exponentially with each additional member of your team.

community@thechangemakergroup.com

Burnout is on the rise. It is a growing problem for the modern workplace, having an impact on organisational costs, as well as employee health and well-being. These include possible long-term health risks and, due to its contagious nature, a toxic working environment of low morale, scapegoating, and increased office politics. The annual cost of burnout to the global economy has been estimated to be £255 billion. Such costs have led to the World Health Organisation predicting a global pandemic within a decade.

In your lifetime, you have learned and developed many skills which allow you to function to the best of your abilities at work and in your home. However, over the past few years the need to build resilience has increasingly been highlighted. To assist you to manage the strain of stress; the attack of constant change; the feeling of the lack of control and the infiltration of being unceasingly overwhelmed, tired or apathetic, this relatively recently identified trait has risen as a 'must have' for you. Your overall well-being and that of any groups of which you are a part, depends on your individual resilience.

What does it mean to be resilient?

If there were two yous - one who wasn't resilient and one who was - these are some of the differences you would see:

The resilient you:

> *Is a you who is able to deal with all the stresses and strains of the modern life.*

> *Is a you who adapts to the changes necessary without it taking a negative toll on you.*

> *Is a you who has 'bounce back' abilities, if life knocks you down, you can return stronger.*

> *Is a you who doesn't wallow in or dwell on your 'failures'.*

> *Is a you who is able to look squarely at the 'reality' of a situation.*

> *Is a you who will look for the 'lessons to be learned' and take them on board.*

> *Is a you who will dust yourself off and get moving forward again as soon as possible.*

> *And is a you who is fully equipped to be wholly committed either at home or at work.*

Being resilient does not mean that you won't experience difficulties or distress. In fact, the most resilient people have often experienced much emotional pain and sadness and may have suffered major adversity or trauma in their lives. The important aspect is that they have carried on despite the ordeal, they have come through stronger than before. Each test of your resilience can strengthen your ability. It is very important for you to know that resilience is not a trait you either have or do not have. It involves behaviours, thoughts, and actions that you can learn and develop with relative ease. In other words, this is not a strategy for avoiding stress: it is a way of efficiently dealing with stress when it comes along.

Your 'bounceability'

One of the inviting definitions of resilience is your 'bounceability'.

If you observe the ball in this illustration, it is beautifully round as it falls and then becomes quite squashed as it impacts with the surface, but then regroups and starts to head back up and to once again become nice and round. In architecture and science, the term resilience has long been used to define the properties of, for example, a metal or in biology, an environmental system. Originating from the Latin verb: 'resaltare' which means to rebound or bounce back it is most commonly used today to mean to adapt to circumstances in the face of some shocking event.

Please note that the ball does get squashed. As do you when something traumatic happens! Being resilient does not mean that you pretend you are fine. It is very important to be sad, angry, confused, depressed as the situation demands. This is healthy and healing. It is another form of energy, one which has often caused great creativity and expression. The big difference with a resilient person is that they KNOW they will not stay there, they will re-inflate and bounce back up again.

At this point it is most important, to mention that if you are reading this you ARE already resilient, and here you may learn some ways to increase your bounceability and overall resilience. More good news is that research has shown you become even more resilient as you age!

2. Resilience foundation

There has been extensive psychological research on this topic over the past 40 years. Beginning with Norman Garmezy, Professor Emeritus of the University of Minnesota in Minneapolis, who studied the children of schizophrenic parents and discovered they did not suffer any psychological illness as a result of growing up with them. Holocaust victims have frequently been mentioned; some of the survivors creating a 'plastic shield'. Their resilience shield comprised: humour – often black; acceptance of reality; a deep belief that life is meaningful and an ability to improvise. One of the best known, Viktor E. Frankl, an Austrian psychiatrist and an Auschwitz survivor, invented "meaning therapy," a humanistic therapy technique that helps individuals make the kinds of decisions that will create significance in their lives. He devised this whilst in the camp.

Salvatore R. Maddi, a psychology professor at the University of California, links resilience training with the term 'hardiness', this is also helping people construct meaning in their everyday lives. He says, "The difference with psychotherapy and resilience training is that psychotherapy is for people whose lives have fallen apart badly and need repair, whereas resilience skills show people life skills and attitudes. Maybe those things should be taught at home, maybe they should be taught in schools, but they're not. So we end up doing it as part of our business training."

Tying in with these concepts, a leading psychologist, Susan Kobasa, mentions three elements essential to resilience:

Challenge – if something goes wrong, is a 'failure' or does not meet expectations, thinking of it as a challenge keeps your brain's door open to look for ways to turn the situation around – often to be better than it was before.

Commitment – having something perceived as 'bigger' than yourself, being passionate, having a purpose, knowing that you do make a positive difference in this world, is a powerful resilience booster.

Control – of yourself, whatever happens about you, you can be in control of your responses. The 8-step routine I will share with you enables you to master these three important aspects and more!

Dean Becker, president and CEO of Adaptive Learning Systems, says "More than education, more than experience, more than training, a person's level of resilience will determine who succeeds and who fails. That's true in the cancer ward, it's true in the Olympics, and it's true in the boardroom."

About eleven years ago, Richard Israel, creator of 'the last four feet' sales technique, and I applied our knowledge of stress management and wellness building strategies to address the problem of business people not having enough time to address the strain they were feeling, let alone, start to build their resilience. After extensive testing and tweaking we created *Mind Chi!*

Mind Chi offers you a simple and revolutionary way to improve your mental energy, regain control, achieve your goals, solve problems; manage the strain of stress and build your resilience, all in just 8-minutes a day. Mind Chi is a synthesis of positive psychology, mental wellness and eudemonics (the study of happiness).

The eight steps of Mind Chi are grounded firmly in established theories of memory, mind and motivational development and are the distillation of over eighty years' combined personal experience and development by the authors. The techniques are designed to improve your control, willpower and focus, and in so doing increase your resilience and overall success in business and life.

Mind Chi is your mental energy: everything that you do, feel, express, experience and think is fueled by your mental energy. Every thought, action or emotion results from the way you direct your energy. Are you using it for your own good or for your self-destruction? Becoming aware of how you are functioning at this moment is the first step to building your overall resilience.

3. Your resilience needs

How resilient do you think you are? These questions bring to your discernment some of the thoughts and behaviours which might help or hinder your resilience.

With the 12 questions below please respond with a yes or no response, if your reply really is sometimes, then please mark on the line. Please complete the two right-hand columns first.

How resilient are you?	YES	NO	YES	NO
	28 days later		Fill in NOW!	
Do you often recall negative episodes?				
Do you resist change in work/life?				
Do you habitually feel you are a victim?				
Do you lack the energy to want to try?				
Do you frequently say 'never' or 'always'?				
Do you have low self-concept/confidence?				
Do you mostly feel in control of yourself?				
Do you stay focussed under pressure?				
Do you bounce back after hardships?				
Do you feel basically 'hopeful'?				
Do you have coping 'strategies'?				
Do you think realistically positively?				

On the following page is an introduction to the 8-steps of the Mind Chi basic routine. It is quite easy to do and requires no special equipment, just 8-minutes where, preferably, you can be uninterrupted. After you have performed the routine for 28 days, answer the resilience questions again, making sure you cover up your previous responses. When you uncover, you can see what differences there might be. Most people see a significant improvement and all for an 8-minute a day investment of time - possibly the best investment you can make for your wellbeing and resilience.

Are you feeling the strain from stress?

If you are not feeling wonderfully resilient, it is also likely that you are suffering the strains of stress. To give you an idea of how you are presently functioning in this arena please complete this short questionnaire. Again, please use the far right-hand column first.

Instructions: Use a scale where 0 = none / negative and 10 = high / perfect!

Questions	28 days later	NOW
How would you rate your energy throughout your work day?		
How much energy do you have at the end of a work day?		
How well are you sleeping?		
How would you rate your memory?		
How would you rate your concentration?		
How is your ability to make choices?		
How clear is your thinking?		
How positive are your 'inner thoughts'?		
How would you rate your self-esteem?		
How well are you managing negative stress?		
How satisfied are you with your work/life balance?		
How is your general health?		

What does this questionnaire reveal about how you are currently using your Mind Chi (mental energy) and how much strain you may be experiencing?

If you are alive you are being constantly stressed; the lights; temperature; sounds; feeling hungry or too full, and then there is whatever may be going on with your family, friends and work mates. Most of the time we manage, taking on more and more, but then cracks start to show as the strain takes its toll. This is when applying the coping strategies you know, can save you from more serious physical or mental suffering.

Instead of being squashed by the strain, the stressors are still there, and you are able to stay fully round and resilient.

On the 'How resilient are you?' questionnaire (page 99), if you responded 'No' to the first 6 questions and 'Yes' to questions 7 – 12, you are showing that you do have a resilient attitude. If you have yeses for the questions 1 – 6 and nos to questions 7 – 12, then you may wish to incorporate some of the suggestions in this chapter.
With the 'Strain from Stress Questionnaire', any number below 5 deserves your attention and some remedial resilience strategies.

4. Your resilience intervention

Resilience is a continuum that includes stress management and also encompasses stress prevention and treatment. One example of the many companies which include resilience training for their staff, is Goldman Sachs, they say, "We define resilience as the state of health, energy, readiness, flexibility, and the capacity to adapt to change with confidence. The goal is to help people perform optimally in both their professional and personal lives."

Here is your functional, easy to do routine to manage the strain you may be feeling and even more importantly, build your resilience for your improved wellbeing.

Mind Chi basic 8-steps

Here is an introduction to the Mind Chi basic 8-minute routine, please follow the overview map below as you experience the steps:

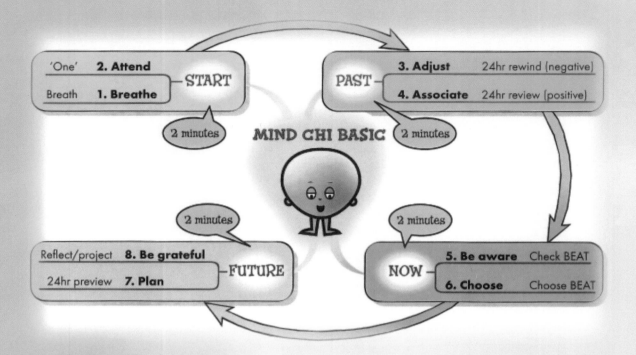

There are four segments to the Mind Chi basic routine, each with two steps, making the 8-minute total.

Start where the branch says 'START' (top left hand)

The first two steps, taking a minute each, cause your body and mind to be set up, under your control and ready for constructive action.

Breathe - Place one hand on your belly and make sure that it rises and falls more than your other hand which is placed high on your chest. Do deep 'belly breaths' for a minute, that is to make a 'square shape' in-hold-out-wait for 3 seconds for each side of the square. This is good to do any time you want to resist the impact of a 'flash stressor'; improve your concentration; think more effectively or solve a problem.

Attend - Look at a second hand on a time piece and think of the word 'One' for a full minute. As soon as an intruding thought comes in, move up a number. Notice what number you reached by the end of the minute. The object is to keep your score at 'one' but more importantly, it is an indicator of how calm or frazzled your mind is at this moment.

The next two steps look at your 'PAST' performance over 24 hours

Adjust - Rewind your mental 'video' to see where you might have acted / spoken / been more helpful. Count these times on your non-dominant hand. This is not to berate yourself, but to look for the lessons, what would you rather have done? Remember the lessons and then let the past be past – let it go.

Associate - Review your mental 'video' again to see where you did perform in a helpful and positive way. Link these with your feelings of success. Count these on your dominant hand. Celebrate and quietly congratulate yourself for all those times when you know you put in the effort. Treasure these as they will tenderly build your self-concept.

The next two steps look at 'NOW'. This is where you can experience (re)gaining control over yourself. Check your BEAT and be in control of you in the 'now'.

Be Aware - Check in with your Body, Emotions, Actions and Thoughts (BEAT) to observe how they are functioning. Perform a quick Body scan, are you holding tension somewhere? Find what Emotions you are experiencing, are they helping what you are doing? What about your Actions, are you using only the amount of energy necessary? And your Thoughts, that voice that chats away in your head, is it building you up or tearing you down?

Choose - Crucial step! Because IF they are not what you wish, this is where you change them! With your Body, stretch or move to release any tension. Pick the Emotion that is most appropriate for what you are doing, put it 'on' as a cloak. Your Actions, consider the amount of energy the task actually requires and adjust as necessary. Become aware of your Thoughts and their influence on you. If they are negative and undermining, check if there is any validity otherwise ask for your positive and supportive voice to speak louder and assist you.

And the final two steps give you the 'FUTURE' you desire.

Plan - Project 24 hours, how would you like to be / act / think and feel? Multi-sensorially experience yourself in a forward 'video'. In many ways research shows that your 'reality' is created in your mind, again project with appropriate optimism to fashion what you do wish rather than what you don't want.

Be Grateful - This is for all that you have received and may receive – during the day register all the small and large things for which you could be grateful, then re-enjoy them in this minute. This is your final step and it sends you on your way with a happy heart, a slight smile on your face, spring in your step and an expectant frame of mind.

And that is how simple it is! However, expect to be delightfully surprised by the power and effectiveness of this 8-minute routine, especially as it builds over time. A business owner came to me on the brink of burnout, additionally her staff were being very difficult and uncooperative. I taught them all Mind Chi, which they incorporated it into the daily office routine. Several years later they are still reaping the benefits.

Mind Chi provides a coping strategy for that impending pandemic and the constant changes of life, most importantly it can build your overall resilience, so that if you must face a tough time, you are as ready as possible to not only survive but thrive!

5. And the role of your temperament?

From the moment you are born you display a temperament and that is the same for any baby anywhere in the world. Knowing and understanding your own basic temperament and disposition is amazingly empowering. You gain an insight as to why you are as you are and it validates your way of experiencing the world. At the same time, it introduces an empathy for why some others, often those very close to you, are different, it is a real eye opener and potential relationship builder. Further, it provides a rationale for why you enjoy doing certain things and are usually good at them, and yet find some other seemingly 'simple' things difficult for you. There is nothing wrong with you! You are being you and now it can be justified. Another empowering aspect is that once you are more aware of your natural strengths and weaknesses, you also know that you are able to stretch into those 'weaker' areas and develop them as necessary, just like a 'muscle'.

For many years, my research focused on discovering why some people were more resilient than others. Why did some coping strategies work for them and not others? Encountering and applying the work of Jung and other researchers of these temperament differences helped me to understand why this was happening.

Programmes such as the Clarity4D program, which identifies four styles of operation and communication: Reflective; Directive; Supportive and Expressive, provide a clear pathway for communication, relationships and teams. This is the basis for the 'Colour me Resilient' programme which applies your temperament to create eight bespoke resilience strategies.

More recently, research by Dr John Mervyn-Smith and Professor Adrian Furnham of the Game Changer Index, (GCI) have identified five basic proclivities or tendencies. Their work specifically targets the 'Game Changers' in organisations and goes on to identify five crucial roles for the completion of any change project, they are: The Game Changer who transforms the future; the Play Maker who orchestrates the future; the Strategist who maps the future; the Implementer who builds the future and the Polisher who creates a future to be proud of.

The Change Maker Group has developed an online profile with GCI, The Change Maker Profile (powered by The GC Index), to apply this to understanding, developing and directing these different proclivities to attain the change your company is desiring. Most importantly, it says that every proclivity is needed at different stages of a project. Everyone has a chance to shine in their moment in the change process. This is very good for building the resilience of every team member, knowing they do have a role and how their part interacts and supports the others to make change happen as desired.

Different coping strategies

My passion is to create easy to do, highly effective processes which can be applied to your life on a daily basis to encourage you to experience it more fully, satisfactorily, positively and enjoyably! To this end you could experience crafting 8 resilience strategies, based on your temperament, to provide an enhancement of your overall resilience and bounceability from a program called 'Colour me Resilient'.

Here are two of the 8-steps for you to experience:

To complete the activity below identify what are resilience suckers. A 'resilience sucker' is a person, activity, place or some other thing that almost as soon as you start to think about them or it, you feel as though all the energy is being sucked out of you. You feel yourself deflate with a soft hiss as you empty of air. It seems that we all have some of these things in our lives. Becoming aware of them, means that you can take steps to balance out your energy and keep yourself properly inflated based on your specific proclivity.

Please write or map below the resilience suckers in your life:

You may wish to start this and leave the page close by as you might discover extra ones as you go through your daily life. Just keep adding them to the appropriate section.

When you have completed your resilience suckers, at least for now, look over them and see if there is just ONE that you may be able to remove? Is there someone who always brings you down who you might let drop out of your life? Or might you analyse what it is about them that is deflating and have a conversation about it?

Several things may then happen: They may have no idea of their impact and want to change it at once, or they may get very cross and wish you goodbye, after sharing a few home truths about you: either way you now have a clear and much more resilient pathway ahead.

Put those negative thoughts aside for a while as we consider the positive side, your resilience boosters. These are the opposite of the suckers, these people, places, activities and things are the ones that help you to pump yourself up, feel re-energised, look at life in a more confident way. Please write or map them below:

As before you may wish to add to this over a few days as you think of others to include. When people complete these maps in my sessions they frequently discover that there are some resilience boosters, that they had forgotten about, friends with whom they had lost touch, places they hadn't been in a while and used to love, for example It can be something as simple as taking a fragrant bath which makes them feel extra special. As you remember boosters, add them to your resilience booster map as they are all very important to build your resilience.

Take a moment to compare your resilience suckers and boosters maps. Do you have more on one than on the other? Which is it? If you have more boosters than suckers then you probably feel happy, keep up the good work, however there is no harm in still looking to see if you can reduce your suckers even further. If, as many people, you have more suckers, then it is important to discover how you can start to balance out your life.

One way is to consciously make time to increase the resilience boosters in your life. The interesting thing is that it does not take that much time, a quick phone call or a special cup of tea, to make a real difference to your entire attitude and therefore your physiology. It is one of the most beneficial investments you can make.

Although this is very personal, looking at your dominant proclivities and pondering how these affects what boosts or reduces your resilience can create a significantly positive move, first for you and then it also impacts the others with whom you work and live.

6. Your action steps:

Transitioning from theory to making that personal, practical, implementable impact in your life requires taking some action steps, select one to start you on your own road to increased resilience.

- Becoming aware is the first step to any action.
- A small shift in thinking or behaviour can create a lasting positive impact.
- Dust off (if necessary) your sense of humour, it creates your resilience shield.
- Look at your situation with your eyes and mind wide open – what is the reality?
- Revisit your purpose in life, why are you here? Relate that to your work.
- Develop your creativity, look for ways to improvise.
- Understand your strengths and how you best function.
- Build your ability to hold the reins of control over yourself – regardless of external factors.

Vanda North is The Change Maker Group's Resilience specialist. Her purpose and passion is to provide easy, practical, brain-compatible processes to help people increase their resilience and joy in life. She is an author and international speaker on these topics. She has also climbed Mt Kilimanjaro, been a bridge tender and loves to garden and bake.

CONFLICT MANAGEMENT – MANAGING DIFFICULT BEHAVIOURS : ARE THESE BEHAVIOURS DIFFICULT OR JUST DIFFERENT?

by Angie Beeston

> Snapshot: Angie Beeston shows why an awareness of potential sources of conflict in change is important; how our mindset can help with managing tensions; and the need for a greater understanding of the importance of our attitude and behaviour and its effects on conflict.

So what is conflict management? A phrase banded around regularly these days. We are living in a world that is so fast paced, technology has raised the expectation of every individual that we should respond NOW. The increase in social media and communication apps created to help us better talk to each other seems ironically to have also developed a darker side. Added to this, we also have to deal with constant change in both our working and personal lives. Change in itself can be a huge factor in creating tension and conflict.

Our expectations are such that we want to know why people are not responding to our emails immediately, so we don't wait. What do most people do if they don't get an instant answer? They send a text, or a messenger comment, Whatsapp, and so on, and so on….

Patience and tolerance seems to be in a much shorter supply in some situations. We see people being irate and reacting emotionally to what may seem like a trivial matter to us.

The downside of this changing expectation levels to responses mean stress can work its way into our everyday life without us even realising it.

Demands from not just our customers, but also our peers, managers and senior leaders create added pressure to us, along with changes in our working conditions, the business, our teams, and so on.

The outcome of all of these hidden and indirect challenges can sometimes mean the cause and effect overspills to become traumatic and a conflict situation is suddenly something we are forced to deal with in our work space.

Definition of Conflict

A serious disagreement and argument about something important. If two people or groups are in conflict, they have had a serious disagreement or argument and have not yet reached an agreement.

(Source: Collins Dictionary)

Conflict Management can also be defined as *MANAGING DIFFICULT BEHAVIOURS.*

The issues we then face are just how do we deal with these situations?

From experience of supporting many leaders and business owners who are suffering due to conflict situations that have arisen, the overriding feeling is one of an 'ostrich head in the sand' moment.. .. "If I ignore it, it will go away….."

Sadly this is often not the case. Ignoring the situation can exacerbate it, turning what was a small issue into a mammoth nightmare, where ultimately HR have to step in and get involved, legal teams are employed and the costs and stress as a result of this are extreme. It then not only involves the directors, owners, leaders but also has a detrimental effect on the rest of the team, over spilling to other departments, and at its worst, like a bad apple can infect the whole organisation.

Leaders are left scratching their heads wondering how they can resolve morale and re-set standards, when things around them are negative, destructive and potentially damaging when good members of staff get so disillusioned, they start to look for another job and the talent is subsequently lost.

Those left behind can become demotivated and potentially damaging for the organisation as normality and perceptions are lost in the conflict situation.

That is why any potential conflict situation, however small it is deemed, needs to be addressed as soon as possible to try and avoid this happening.

Sources of Conflict:

Conflict can arise from many sources and sometimes seems to come from nowhere catching us by surprise:

Internal - our colleagues, managers, other departments, different divisions, stakeholders

External - our customers, legislative bodies, Government departments, sponsors

Therefore a challenging situation, high expectations from external sources mixed with demands from internal sources can create potentially harmful conflict.

Let's take each one in turn.

Internal Conflict:

Our business needs to be more profitable, our resources are reduced, costs need to be driven down, managers are asked (or told) to take on more work….. sound familiar?

The results of these pressures will test the best of us and our own resilience (see Vanda North's chapter on resilience) to managing stressful situations.

Some individuals will seemingly take on additional pressures without demonstrating any negative behaviours or attitudes at all.   On the flip side, there will be others who are unable to deal with this and will actively express their feelings.   In both cases, as a manager, our ultimate challenge is to try and deal with both aspects.   Those individuals who don't express their feelings shouldn't be ignored as everyone has their breaking point.

So what can cause conflict internally?

Causes of Conflict:

According to psychologists Art Bell and Brett Hart, there are eight common causes of conflict in the workplace. Bell and Hart identified these common causes in separate articles on workplace conflict in 2000 and 2002.

You can use this classification to identify possible causes of conflict. Once you've identified these, you can take steps to prevent conflict happening in the first place, or you can tailor your strategy to fit the situation.

community@thechangemakergroup.com

1. Conflicting Resources

We all need access to certain resources – whether these are office supplies, help from colleagues, or even a meeting room – to do our jobs well. When more than one person or group needs access to a particular resource, conflict can occur.

2. Conflicting Styles

Everyone works differently, according to his or her individual needs and personality. For instance, some people love the thrill of getting things done at the last minute, while others need the structure of strict deadlines to perform. However, when working styles clash, conflict can often occur.

3. Conflicting Perceptions

All of us see the world through our own lens, and differences in perceptions of events can cause conflict, particularly where one person knows something that the other person doesn't know, but doesn't realise this.

If your team members regularly engage in "turf wars" or gossip, you might have a problem with conflicting perceptions. Additionally, negative performance reviews or customer complaints can also result from this type of conflict.

4. Conflicting Goals

Sometimes we have conflicting goals in our work. For instance, one of our managers might tell us that speed is the most important goal with customers. Another manager might say that in-depth, high-quality service is the top priority. It's sometimes quite difficult to reconcile the two!   This can often be the case when there are blurred lines in chains of command and individuals have multiple managers.

Whenever you set goals for your team members, make sure that those goals don't conflict with other goals set for that person, or set for other people.

5. Conflicting Pressures

We often have to depend on our colleagues to get our work done. However, what happens when you need a report from your colleague by noon, and he's already preparing a different report for someone else by that same deadline?

Conflicting pressures are similar to conflicting goals; the only difference is that conflicting pressures usually involve urgent tasks, while conflicting goals typically involve projects with longer timelines.

6. Conflicting Roles

Sometimes we have to perform a task that's outside our normal role or responsibilities. If this causes us to step into someone else's "territory," then conflict and power struggles can occur. The same can happen in reverse – sometimes we may feel that a particular task should be completed by someone else.

Conflicting roles are similar to conflicting perceptions. After all, one team member may view a task as his or her responsibility or territory. But when someone else comes in to take over that task, conflict occurs.

7. Different Personal Values

Imagine that your boss has just asked you to perform a task that conflicts with your ethical standards. Do you do as your boss asks, or do you refuse? If you refuse, will you lose your boss's trust, or even your job?

When our work conflicts with our personal values like this, conflict can quickly arise.

8. Unpredictable Policies

When rules and policies change at work and you don't communicate that change clearly to your team, confusion and conflict can occur.

In addition, if you fail to apply workplace policies consistently with members of your team, the disparity in treatment can also become a source of dissension.

(Source: Bell & Hart)

Taking into consideration all these areas of potential conflict, no matter how experienced we are as a leader, it is inevitable we will have to deal with conflict and difficult behaviours at some point.

External Conflict:

This could involve customers, legislation, Government bodies, Sponsors, key stakeholders and so on. What causes conflict for them?

community@thechangemakergroup.com

High expectations, consumer pressure leading to impatience, urgent actions needed. It may be previous situations where individuals have had bad experiences which result in perceived aggressive behaviour being displayed.

All these can lead to this group of people wanting and demanding answers NOW from our teams.

Understanding sources of conflict and putting ourselves into the shoes of others can go a long way in trying to defuse and calm the situation.

If we take an empathetic view towards these challenging situations, often we can calm things before they accelerate into something more serious.

The ability to put our mind into the 'right' mode allows us to think clearly before reacting – this is the ultimate goal to responding to conflict situations.

Handling Internal Conflict:

Speaking to many managers and senior directors, managing conflict is one of the most difficult areas they find to deal with. They get frustrated by the seeming pettiness, yet not dealing with it at the start may create far more difficulties for everyone.

As mentioned before, staff morale could be destroyed and having to improve the atmosphere is very time consuming and draining for all.

Case Studies:

Take some of these examples of conflict I have dealt with to support my clients, and how they were approached:

Conflict Situation	Approach/Solution	Outcome
Manager (Ruth) and assistant carer (Jane)		
Jane opened a door quickly when Ruth was walking along with a trolley of hot drinks. Ruth shouted out "be careful!" to alert Jane. Ruth then spoke to Jane "that was a stupid thing to do, you need to be careful". Jane took offence and escalated the complaint to the senior director. An HR investigation was undertaken, with witness and character statements made, 2 x 40 page reports were written from both sides. No further action was deemed necessary but the fallout from the conflict resulted in the manager and carer struggling to work together on their shifts. This started to affect the whole team.	As the two individuals involved were scarred by the experience, particularly Ruth who felt she had been harassed and unfairly treated, mediation was offered to try and reach a compromise and defuse the pain. Both parties were offered external 1-1 coaching support to explore ways of managing the relationships moving forwards.	The two individuals were given tools and ways to handle the situation when they were on the same shift. Trust was damaged but there were some elements that slowly started to be rebuilt. The two were never going to be best friends but both were encouraged that they could find a mutually beneficial compromise of working together for the purpose of doing a very good job and not jeopardising company standards.

Conflict Situation	Approach/Solution	Outcome
Director (Elaine) and Assistant Manager (Jeff)		
Elaine was struggling to manage Jeff as she felt he was not able to set professional boundaries with his small team. He had issues with favouritism with those he socialised with and seemed to side with the team rather than support management decisions. Jeff was argumentative (in the eyes of Elaine) and seemed to be constantly behaving in a difficult manner. Elaine was drained with the effort of managing him and the fallout from his lack of management skills.	By working to support Jeff and Elaine over a period of time, both of the individuals were encouraged to change their approach to try and reach a resolution to stop the perceived favouritism. Ways to set professional boundaries were discussed and changes monitored. Elaine needed to understand why Jeff seemed to be being difficult. Through open communication, it transpired Jeff had had a problem where supposed confidential meetings had been openly discussed with others in the senior management team, breaking promises and trust. This had to be rebuilt and relationships re-established.	Elaine and Jeff both worked hard to re-build trust over time, putting their differences aside and enabling them to get back on track working together. This allowed the atmosphere for the rest of the team and organisation to calm and provide a much better working environment for all.

Conflict Situation	Approach/Solution	Outcome
Senior director (Liz), Manager (Justine), team member (Bob)		
Justine was promoted from team leader to manager but the senior director was concerned about Justine's ability to manage one of the team members, Bob. Justine and Bob were close friends and they regularly socialised together. Bob took advantage of the relationship by refusing to do certain tasks, not turning up for shifts, questioning every request and making life hard for the other team members. As a result, Liz had to deal with 6 members of staff who left because of his attitude and Justine's inability to deal with the situation. Liz wanted to develop the whole team and was very concerned not just with all the staff who had felt they had to leave, but also Justine's behaviour and attitude having a detrimental effect on the other managers.	A bespoke Managing Difficult Behaviours workshop was run for the whole team. The thought process was to set standards and remind everyone of the need and importance of understanding others and dealing with challenging situations. Team activities were included to raise awareness of how others may see us and to explore self-awareness of our own impact. 1-1 support was offered to Justine to talk through management styles and professional approaches.	Justine's new awareness of her impact was initially very uncomfortable as she needed to find a level where she could re-set standards, without being seen as a 'weak' leader. Through the 1-1 support and constructive feedback, she developed her skills to enable her to manage the team in a very professional manner, whilst still being respected by all individuals.

Taking all this into consideration, how do we deal with it?

It can be very easy to place the blame of a difficult interaction with the other person as we can often be clouded by our own opinion and perceptions. Sometimes we are too close to an issue. This can make it hard to rationalise and causes a conflict for us. It is important to try and take a moment to consider things from a clear perspective and focus on where the other person might be coming from. This will help you to manage the situation. It is also important to try and establish the best approach to deal with a scenario based on another's viewpoint.

Our Two Minds

We operate with two fundamental ways of knowing the world – a rational mind and an emotional mind.

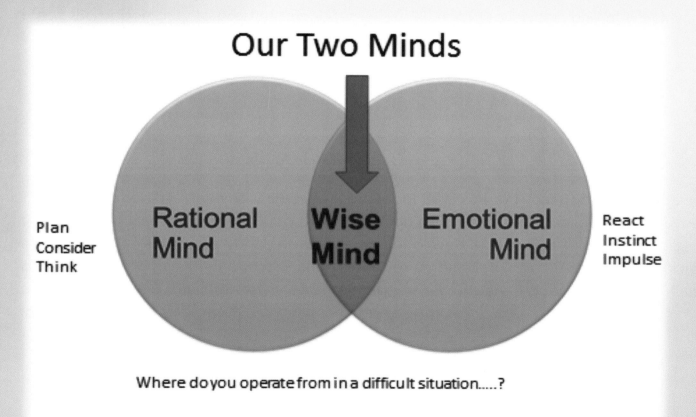

The rational mind is the way we make sense of the world and the one we use most often in everyday life. It is the mind we use consciously to understand, reason, ponder and reflect upon things that happen to us. We use it to consider and make decisions and think through and understand the consequences of our actions.

The emotional mind is by contrast a more impulsive, powerful and sometimes illogical way of knowing. It is our response to the more emotional side of our experience: driven by states like anger, fear, happiness and grief.

For the most part these two minds operate in harmony with each other intertwining these two different ways of knowing to help us develop a full understanding of our world and experiences. The two minds are kept in balance: our emotions feeding into and informing the rational mind and the rational refining, making sense and sometimes vetoing the emotional mind.

The third place our mind operates is the Wise Mind – think of this as a PAUSE button for your brain!

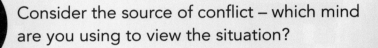

Consider the source of conflict – which mind are you using to view the situation?

More importantly, which mind is the other person using?

This is very important to try and reach compromise positions – understanding where we are sitting and where the other person is.

When emotions surge the balance between logical and emotional can be tipped and the emotional mind becomes predominant. The more intense the emotion the more dominant the emotional mind becomes – and the more ineffectual the rational.

In practical terms – the effect of this imbalance means we have to be very specific about which mind we are appealing to when dealing with someone who is strongly driven by his or her emotional mind. Resolving the issue or problem will undoubtedly require the use of the rational mind, which has become eclipsed by the emotional mind. If we try to reason with the person, show him or her why something cannot logically be true or explain the reasons why something has or hasn't happened, it will have little impact upon the individual and may even serve to increase his or her emotional state. It is important to appeal to the emotional mind by using interactions that

community@thechangemakergroup.com

will serve to reduce the strong emotion – thus allowing the rational mind to become more effective.

Emotional hijack

There are occasions when we react quickly to an incident – only to find that it was not as it seemed to be. Sometimes this can be as simple as thinking you are alone in the house and jumping suddenly when someone walks in to the room, then realising that it is your partner.

The reason for this 'emotional hijack' is down to the way we process information. Visual and auditory information are sent to the *thalamus*. A signal is then sent across a single synapse to the *amygdala* (the emotional mind) and a second signal is routed to the *neocortex* (the rational mind), which processes it at several levels before it fully perceives the situation. All this happens in milliseconds but the resulting gap means we react emotionally first and the rational mind catches up to let us know what the reality of the situation is.

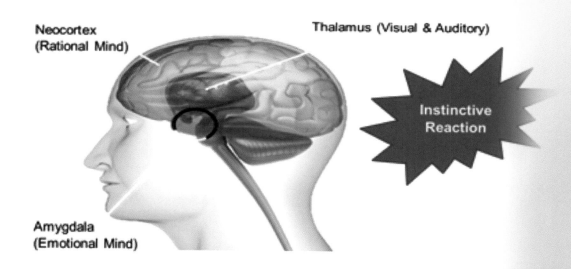

Consider what happens when someone who is rational tries to pacify /explain /discuss something with someone who has become emotional.   Can the conversation get anywhere?

How do you think you should respond?

What may be the best thing to do if one is emotional and the other is rational?

You could look to take a break; arrange a meeting or conversation for another time; say "I can see you are upset/angry now, but where would you like to get to/what would you like to achieve by the end of this meeting?" Or ask: "This is clearly upsetting you, how do you want to take this forward?"

The Attitude and Behaviour Cycle

It is extremely unlikely that you will have a positive attitude towards everyone you meet in the course of your work. Some people, for any number of reasons, will cause you to have negative feelings towards them. If you are dealing with someone you feel negative towards, you are likely to show those negative feelings in the way that you behave towards the person.

When the other person recognises this negative behaviour from you, this will in turn affect their attitude towards you. A negative attitude will come out in their behaviour towards you. Their negative behaviour is then likely to reinforce your original negative feelings and make your feelings even more negative. This is shown in the Attitude and Behaviour Cycle.

It is very difficult to instantly change your attitude towards someone. It is however possible to change the way you behave towards them. You can learn to behave so that your feelings do not show, so that your behaviour doesn't reflect your negative feelings. This breaks the cycle and stops it getting worse.

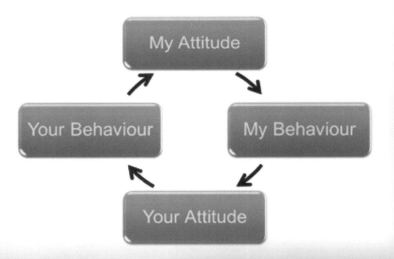

People often are quite adamant that attitude is easier to change than behaviour and it can become an issue in a group. The misconception stems from the fact that to change your attitude is the *best* way of breaking the cycle and groups often go for it because of this – but in practice it's extremely difficult to do so quickly.

community@thechangemakergroup.com

Our attitudes (which include our beliefs and values) are formed over a long period of time and we cannot just change them overnight. If we don't like a particular type of person, or group of people – it is based on our attitude towards them, or their beliefs, or the way they behave. People are unlikely to change their attitudes, and will see no reason for doing so, unless they have experiences that suggest that their attitude may not be right. And this change will only happen over time.

Behaviour, on the other hand, is directly within our control and we can choose (within limits) the behaviour that we use towards anyone. No matter how strong the attitude (even if it is prejudiced) – everyone has the ability to behave in an appropriate way towards those they do not agree with.

So it is easier to change behaviour than attitude. It is *more effective* in the long term to change attitude. The attitude-behaviour cycle can have a positive effect. If your attitude towards someone is negative, but you control your behaviour to be positive – then if the other person is friendly and positive back this is likely to make you examine your attitude. If you get enough positive experiences then you will eventually change your attitude.

Throughout any conflict situation, it is vital that we maintain our standards and don't let others affect our reputation or damage the good work we have already done.

7 Key Considerations to manage Conflict:

Think about your own mindset – where is it?   Emotional, Rational or Wise?

Consider the other person's perspective – how are they viewing the situation?

Prepare – prepare – prepare – to give the most appropriate response

Causes of Conflict – remember everyone's perception and reality is different to ours

Be aware of the impact of your own prejudices and perceptions

Think about your voice, tone and body language – managing your communication styles in a conflict environment is vital

PAUSE button – before reacting, even if you only have seconds, this allows your rational and wise mind to kick in before emotions take over!

We know Change is a constant, but just because we have change does not mean it should create tension and conflict. We need to develop ways of dealing with Change without too much drama.

A thought to leave you with –

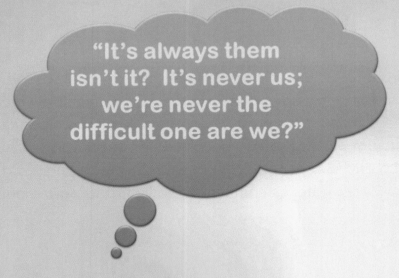

"It's always them isn't it? It's never us; we're never the difficult one are we?"

Or are we…..?

So prepare how to deal with situations, be confident to tackle them, listen, think, reflect and use your Wise Mind before responding.

Good luck!

Diagrams are copyright of © Evolution 4 Business Ltd ®

Angie Beeston is a business mentor and leadership & management specialist, creating and delivering bespoke leadership programmes. She works across many varying sectors to develop and support key strategic objectives and achieve goals. Angie has a wide range of experience in the areas of employee engagement and business strategy. Very early in the morning Angie can often be found swimming in the sea near Bournemouth.

WHY GENDER BIAS IS 'NORMAL' AND WHAT YOU DO ABOUT IT

by Nicky Carew

> Snapshot: Britain has some of the most strict diversity rules in the world – and yet we seem to make little headway to gender equality in pay and opportunity. Nicky Carew explores the reasons and what each of us can do to influence it.

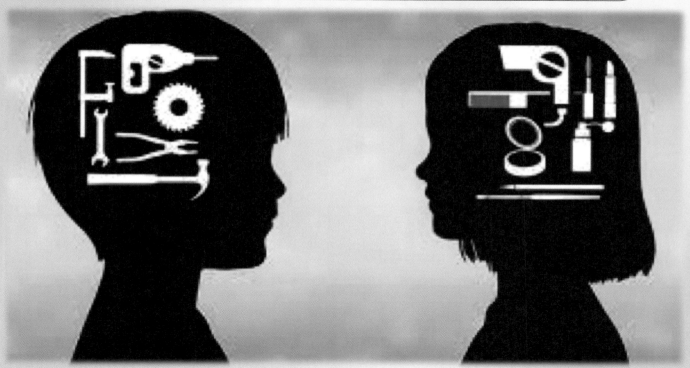

Despite many initiatives to enable women to be more represented in organisations the gender gap is as real as ever. Women are underrepresented at all levels of corporate life, the higher up the corporate ladder the more pronounced it is. The change we hoped for hasn't happened.

When women discuss this with me they use more visceral language: they don't seem to have a voice in their organisation; they tell me that despite resolving potentially damaging conflicts in a team their contribution is overlooked; they report that they seem to be relied on to take notes or help someone out while others, usually men, carve their own self-serving path and are rewarded despite it having detriment to the team.

The focus of this piece is to discuss the biases and frustrations that are experienced daily by people in the workplace and how we can take some control of it. In these cases often the 'offender' is unaware of what they are causing. It shouldn't happen and the impact can be unequal promotion or pay to the detriment of both the women and the organisation. This is, of course, is not on the level of the current shocking revelations of harassment in the media (and widely shared through #metoo). That level of overtly unprofessional behaviour must be dealt with corporately which we will only touch on here, or taken to the police when a criminal act is alleged.

Here we are looking at how can we take control of our own change. We have 5 strategies to make sure that you are less likely to be a victim of gender bias (and these may be appropriate for other diversity issues too). But first we need to understand what is causing gender bias to be stubbornly present.

Implicit Bias (or Unconscious Bias) – we are the result of our experiences, especially from childhood, and these leave subconscious biases, you may have been bullied by someone called Kim and forever you have hated that name. Implicit bias is the attitudes and stereotypes that effect how we see others at a *subconscious* level. So we know intellectually that men and women in the workplace are equal but still nominate a women as better able to take notes at a meeting. Implicit bias has the result of directing us towards flawed judgement when making decisions.

And others with similar biases can reinforce these behaviours – Actor Geena Davis reported that, in family friendly films, of the characters that have jobs 81% of them are men [1].

In other research using actors in work situations we see that people warmed to women in the workplace so long as she was behaving in a neutral or agreeable way. But when defending her point of view forcefully the woman was seen as losing their temper and not in control. The consequence of this is that their perceived competency drops by 35% and their salary reflects this. In men similar aggression results in a perceived competency drop of only 22% [2].

community@thechangemakergroup.com

If you want to see how implicit bias impacts on you then Harvard University have a fascinating test as part of their Project Implicit[3] that you can take to see where your own implicit bias lies.

Corporate Institutional Bias – Technical competence, autonomous action, linear thinking and competitiveness are all typically 'masculine' traits and are all highly valued. Empathy, enabling and collaboration and creating trust are seen as feminine. They are valued, but are not easily measurable and rarely take any role in the reward or salary process. Most corporate systems are not designed to take these qualities into account. Being quietly competent may be interpreted as not being competent at all. Worse still, implicit bias can mean they can be considered to be traits that are innately female so 'just what they do'.

Victoria Coren (before the Mitchell was added) eloquently responded to the apparently obvious statement that as few women appear in the top 500 earners in poker, they just don't have what it takes. This, the speaker extrapolated, meant they weren't competitive enough for big business. Coren, with her usual wit, was able to demolish this fuzzy thinking [4]. Simply put, the measure of success (gross earnings) in poker is not balanced against losses. In her experience women are less gung ho, they don't risk all but come away with healthy profit more consistently. But, like in business, the ballsy operators, who are most likely to be men, make a greater impression.

So, what can you do about it?

Well firstly recognising the impact of implicit bias is a positive step. Automatic reactions don't necessarily make a good judgement. If you are on the receiving end of gender bias there are some practical things to practice.

Naming and Norming:

Don't assume that something you have done to impact on productivity (helped a peer, mentored a team member, tidied up a report) will be respected as having value. Don't leave it to chance how it will be interpreted. Use positive language to interpret it, such as in response to

That was a nice thing to do to help Nick make his report look good.

make it clear that it was your intentional action that increase effectiveness:

What that report needed to get its message over effectively was a strong communicator's skill.

These may seem like small wins but they challenge deep rooted biases.

By consistently offering a different alternative to the old norm you help create a new norm. Each time you clearly make a case for how your (or someone else's) contribution enabled success the stronger the case will get and the more people will commit.

Negotiating:

If you want your style of working to be integrated into the work plan then it will help to get it valued from the beginning by repositioning it into the task. This will require voicing how it will impact an outcome and negotiating your role. If you are asked to do something that confirms gender bias then you will need to avoid seeming awkward – remember that this bias may have came from their unconscious. Rather you would better get your position accepted by showing how much better you could add to the success.

Framing:

The same research on perceived aggression in women above showed that this negative effect can be countered if women frame their statement so that people did not make the judgement that they were out of control or being antagonistic. So before making a forceful point signal to the receiver that you have clear and thoughtful intentions – so *I want to make an important point to make it clear where I stand* – indicates that you are in control and forcefulness is a virtue. This can reduce the backlash by as much as 16%.

Networking:

Many formalised networking activities do not suit women – in their timing or their how they are run. Forming connections is important and you may have to create your own way to do this, women often have their own networks, both formal and informal, on and offline, to exchange career advice and other intelligence. And if you can't make a standard evening networking session make sure you let the people who matter see that you would have liked to catch up with them at another time over coffee.

community@thechangemakergroup.com

Organisational:

Organisations taking this problem seriously should be looking to get their leadership to recognise it and verbalise it. Male dominated senior management teams may be blind to gender bias but when discussed openly many are able to empathise. Even stronger than the business case, often the eye opener is when they realise that unless there is culture change this would be happening to their daughters too.

I recommend that organisations examine their culture when rewarding high-performers and risk-takers without regard to otherwise intolerable behaviour - sexual harassment allegations can be a sign of even more serious violations at a company as the behaviour of self-entitlement spills over into other areas of business life.

Small changes can make a big difference. Make networking situations more gender neutral and start to value the different qualities women bring. When was the last time at an appraisal you were asked "What have you done to help other people achieve their goals?"

As recent history in the banking industry so clearly illustrates being a high-risk taker may look courageous and give high gains, but as in poker, the real stayer is not the most competitive but the most clever.

[1] Geena Davis Institute on Gender and Media

[2] White paper: Emotion Inequality: Skills to Minimize Social Backlash, Joseph Grenny and David Maxfield

[3] Project Implicit, https://implicit.harvard.edu/implicit/takeatest.html

[4] http://www.theguardian.com/commentisfree/2013/aug/25/women-poker-players-financial-crisis

Nicky Carew has over 30 years' experience of working with senior executives to develop their skills to manage in an increasingly complex environment and has a Masters in Executive Coaching. She lives on the site of 1066 Battle of Hastings and still gets excited by rainbows, watching the International Space Station go overhead and meteor showers.

MANAGING YOUR CAREER DURING CHANGE

by Cathy Summers

Snapshot: Wondering what your organisation's changes have in store for you? Are you feeling a bit powerless, or sitting back and hoping for the best? Cathy Summers offers tips to get back into the driving seat, craft a plan that inspires you, make yourself more marketable and keep on top of your game so that you can make the next chapter of your life and career happen.

Change is a constant nowadays. Across all sectors, organisations are on a continuous journey of development and change. Restructure, job change, redeployment and redundancy are all a common part of working life as organisations grow, shrink or reinvent themselves.

Which means that leading change is now integral to most leadership and management job roles. If you're leading and managing people, this includes helping your staff to navigate ongoing change and to manage the personal and professional impact of change.

All very well, but what often gets left behind here is the important task of proactively managing your own career. If you're clear about what you want and you can see that the changes are going to work in your favour, that's great. But if you're uncertain about what you want, it can be hard to know what to do and how to take advantage of any opportunities that come up along the way, internal or external. You may think "I'll just wait and see what happens" - sometimes this is a good tactic, but not always.

"Your career is your business.
It's time for you to manage it as a CEO"

Dorit Sher, CEO of Experity

It's all too easy to lose yourself in the demands of day-to-day working life / home life, meeting the needs and expectations of those around you. The risk is that you leave it too late and the actions you then take are driven by stress, frustration, desperation or panic; knee-jerk responses rather than strategic and informed decisions.

So, if significant changes are on the horizon, what can you do to proactively manage your career through change and avoid 'drift'?

Firstly, take stock. How did you get to be here? Is this where you want to be? What do you want from the next stage of your career – and life?

Sometimes we drift on for years, staying in a job we don't really enjoy, perhaps taking the easier path rather than pursuing the dream we once cherished, not going after what we really want out of uncertainty, fear, or simply being overwhelmed by day-to-day responsibilities.

I can't stress enough how important it is to ask the 'what do I really want' questions of yourself first. It can be tempting to rush into trying to make decisions without taking stock of where you are now and what you want. Whatever your story and your aspirations, there are many insights to be gained from looking back before looking forward. These insights may help you to tap into recurring themes of aspirations or thinking and behaviour patterns, to find valuable clues or perhaps avoid repeating past mistakes.

Here are a few things to think about:

Allow for the possibility that the person you were 5, 10 or 15 years ago may not be the person you are now. Your circumstances may well have changed and likewise your hopes, fears and priorities.

Check if your vision for your life is up to date. Think wider than your job role. Consider what you want from the next chapter/s of your life and how you want the next stage of your career / work to contribute to this.

Take out your old dreams, dust them off and hold them up for inspection. Are they still as important to you now? If not, beware of doggedly pursuing former aspirations just because you haven't achieved them and ticked them off your list yet.

Reflect on what matters to you, what are your motivators / drivers, what kind of work do you want to be doing (e.g. hands on, strategy, planning, advising, building relationships?), what kind of environment do you thrive in (e.g. location, physical environment, culture / atmosphere, how busy or quiet?), and what kind of people do you like to work with. Who is your 'tribe' i.e. the people who share your values, who 'get' you, are good to work with and to be around? Will the 'new world' be a good fit for you?

It may be a while since you thought about any of this and it can take time to think it through. It may feel strange, indulgent or overwhelming to be asking yourself what you want, especially if you're accustomed to looking after everyone else around you or in the habit of "I'll just wait and see..". If you're struggling with these questions, there is advice further on for dealing with internal barriers.

What if I'm thinking about doing something completely different? If you're considering a change of direction, there are a number of tried and tested steps that will help you. These are beyond the scope of this short chapter, so for now here are a few tips to get you off the starting blocks.

"Tell me, what is it you plan to do with your one wild and precious life?"

Mary Oliver, Pulitzer prize-winning American poet

Firstly, decide what kind of life you want (short term or longer term) and map out as much as you know. Don't worry about the bits you don't yet know, you can work on them. Your change of career / work may be a new career direction, perhaps you want to be a change maker in a different arena, or perhaps your future work is going to be a means of financing a bigger game plan for your life.

If you're stuck on working out what you want, try starting with what you don't want. Or try the fairy godmother question "If I could wave a magic fairy wand, what would I like to be doing?". Another good question is "If I couldn't fail, what would I be doing?" Be as honest as you can with yourself here.

Do your maths - what do you need to bring in annually to cover your financial obligations? And what figure would enable you to enjoy life and pursue your other goals and priorities, for example taking holidays, a gap year, buying that new bike, going to the cinema / pub / theatre when you want to? These two figures will give you financial parameters within which to create and explore options.

Be seen as integral to the future. Whether you know what you want or you're still working on it - and however frustrating things are at work - take care to manage your reputation with the same professionalism that you manage your job and your other priorities. This is not about compromising your values or becoming a self-promoting bore.

community@thechangemakergroup.com

It's about being clear about how you would like to be perceived by those around you and conducting yourself accordingly.

"Be so good they can't ignore you"

Steve Martin, actor and comedian

Here are some things to consider:

The world of work has changed and what employers are looking for has changed too. Employees are expected to manage themselves; lead and manage change; manage projects; be highly productive, resilient, manage stress; constantly learn and re-learn; take ownership of their development etc. Know your strengths *and* which of these your current / future employer will most value. Make time for horizon scanning, noticing trends, up-skilling yourself and keeping up to date.

Bear in mind that what made you successful in your current role (or career so far) may be different to what's needed for the next step you're planning to take. For example, if you're planning to move from operational to strategic management, from technical specialist to a broader functional role. Of course you will have many transferable skills, but my point is - look ahead and know what a successful leader in the future world looks like.

You may need to ask some tough questions of yourself. How is your leadership perceived, is your style a good fit for now and for what's coming? Ask for feedback.

Offer to lead or work on a project that will refresh your skills; add to your skills, knowledge or experience; add to your track record of achievement; raise your profile and thereby increase your internal and / or external marketability. Look for opportunities that align with your preferred direction of travel.

Set yourself up for success. Put your project manager hat on, treat this as a work project and afford it the same rigour and self-discipline. This means scheduling time in your diary for it – not just for 'doing', but for thinking time too. You may have to make assumptions about how much time you will need to take the steps above, and you may need to modify these as you go along. However, a rough campaign plan is better than no plan!

Be realistic and honest with yourself about when you will be able to allocate time to the steps above. Use your professional skills to plan, do and review. Build in an accountability plan for yourself (which could include incentives and rewards) or get a friend or colleague to hold you accountable.

Set yourself goals and milestones. Research shows that people who set goals for themselves around what they want are statistically more likely to achieve them. As well as being SMART goals, make sure they are inspiring or you will keep finding excuses not to do them.

Make time to network, internally and externally. Your network can be your marketing team (hence it pays to know what you want).

Equip yourself for the journey. Build a support network of people who are behind you, will champion you, be a sounding board / critical friend, or simply give you some light relief when you need it. Spend sufficient time with these people, especially when times are tough. Look after yourself emotionally and physically, and try to spend more time with the 'sustainers' than the 'drainers' (these may be people, environments, or activities).

If you're planning a change of direction, your nearest and dearest may not be your biggest supporters. This can be a shock and is easy to take personally. Even if they share your dream (and they may not), they will probably be anxious and concerned for you and possibly worried about the impact of any changes on you / them / the family etc. This may show up as questioning, criticism or complete avoidance. It can be hard to deal with this, especially with a fragile or dearly cherished dream, so try to understand what's behind it and keep communicating.

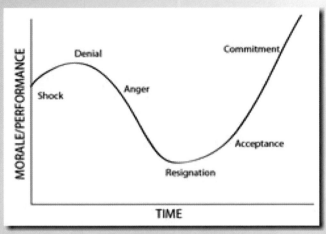
The Kubler-Ross Change Curve

Dealing with internal barriers. How people respond to change is well researched and documented. If you're familiar with the 'change curve' (see diagram) you'll know that people's responses to change (regardless of how smart, capable or senior they are) may include shock, denial, anger and a sense of hopelessness.

If you're in a state of shock or disbelief about what is happening at work, you're unlikely to be in the right frame of mind to work out what you want from the next stage of your working life.

community@thechangemakergroup.com

Also, as we try to make sense of what is going on around us, we sometimes distort the information (consciously or unconsciously) and slip into unhelpful thinking patterns and use of language.

For example:

All or nothing thinking, seeing things as black or white, right or wrong *"I didn't get the last job I applied for, so there's no point in going for another"*. *"If they don't agree to my proposal it will have been a complete waste of time"*

Over-generalising, *"These type of restructures never work..."* *"People my age don't get opportunities like that"*

Being over-dramatic, catastrophising, *"I haven't got a Prince 2 qualification so I'll never be able to move into project management"*

'Shoulds' and 'oughts' *"I ought to go for that job"* *"They ought to have known I wouldn't like that"*

Making assumptions, jumping to conclusions through mind-reading or fortune-telling *"My boss will never agree to me doing a secondment"*, *"The Board rejected my last proposal so they won't agree to this one"*, *"I'm too old to change direction"*

Ignoring the positives and focusing on the negative *"That isn't anything special, anyone could have done it"*

Blaming *"If I was younger / older I would have got that job..."*

"If my parents hadn't made me go into accountancy I could have done something I really wanted to do"

Feelings = facts, if I feel it then it must be true. *"I feel bad about saying that. He won't take me seriously again."* *"I'm scared of failing, I'm bound to get it wrong"* *"I feel guilty"* (it must be my fault)

Your thinking patterns and your language offer valuable clues about your underlying beliefs and values. For example, if your thinking and language is peppered with 'shoulds' and 'oughts', you probably have underlying beliefs around your own / others' expectations of you. This may hold you back from acknowledging what *you* really want and blind you to the options for action that might just get you what you want.

We're all experts in spotting these thinking patterns and habits in others, but it's not always so easy to recognise in ourselves!

Notice and accept where you are on the change curve and treat yourself as you would others. For example, if you are experiencing shock, denial or anger, then give yourself time to adjust.

Master your inner psychology by tackling unhelpful thinking patterns, limiting beliefs and verbal habits. The first step is spotting them – catching yourself doing it. If you can do this and mentally step back for a moment, you will be better able to choose what you say or think.

Reframe negatives into positives. For example, you could reframe "I don't have time to even think about my career development" into "If my team see me putting time and energy into managing my career, it will give them permission to do the same - and I'll be role modeling taking ownership of my personal and professional development."

In summary

Know what you want

Know what employers need and value

Know how to make yourself more marketable

Manage your career like a professional

Set yourself up for success

Cathy Summers specialises in coaching people on career development, career transition and career change. She has changed her own career direction several times and has worked in the private, public and not-for-profit sectors, before starting her business 12 years ago. Cathy lives near Shaftesbury in Dorset and enjoys nipping down to the coast for beach walks, sea breezes and beach cafes.

community@thechangemakergroup.com

WHY WE SHOULD ALL INVEST TIME IN REFLECTIVE LEARNING

by Nicky Carew

Snapshot: In an increasingly complex world we need better, collective problem solving. But traditional learning and reward processes in organisations can actually result in superficial results that waste opportunities for growth and success. Nicky Carew shows how to create a culture of learning that instils better problem solving and collective learning.

"We do not learn from experience… we learn from reflecting on experience."

John Dewey (American philosopher, psychologist and educational reformer)

I wonder what you are going to think about this essay? You may be wondering if reading this will be worth the investment of your time. Being reflective is part of a naturally curious mind. Reflection is an internal process – thinking about and reviewing what has happened or what might happen, what are the issues that have impacted that happening. Sometimes we call it "mulling it over".

When we are young we are learning voraciously – eager to fill a blank canvass. Now that canvass is full of facts, influences, attitudes, experiences and beliefs. We have to pick our way through to choosing the most useful information in any situation. Reflection allows us to examine, to review, to evaluate, to assess, to question our choices.

Without reflection we would be condemned to repeating the same thing over and over again or to follow other people's agendas or perceived wisdom. With reflection we are able to be conscious of and take responsibility for our actions.

Why is this important to me in change?

The time when most of us actively reflect are when things go wrong, or when we have been surprised by something – we feel we have to reconsider or think through that event – they are triggers for reflection – we are impelled to wonder why and to review our old way of thinking. Inevitably, we will learn from this.

Research[1] now shows how important reflection is in both individual learning and organisational development. By comparing the outcome of the classic methods of 'learning by doing' which fosters progress over time with repetition, but now adding the element of thinking through what you have been doing and articulating the lessons, there are significant performance benefits of the latter.

When individuals and organisations are compelled to be more agile to compete in volatile and complex environments we need to see how we can encourage and develop the habit of reflection.

If you are a high achiever, a reflective habit may be even harder for you.

Productive reflection is too important to be left to chance. In fact, most people are resistant to reflective learning. In Teaching Smart People How To Learn[2] Chris Argyris shows how the high flyers, who have a history of success, find learning harder. They simply do not fail enough and the stakes when they do fail are high. The natural response to this situation – in its most basic state a threat – is to rationalise the problem, this is defensive reasoning. If the brief had been clearer we would not have failed or the clients moved the goal posts... there is always a solid reason why projects fail. Whereas Argylis does not doubt the individuals' commitment to continuous improvement, as shown by their beliefs and what they say (espoused theory), in fact their actual behaviour serves to block continuous improvement. What can you do if the client moves the goal post!

community@thechangemakergroup.com

How do most high achievers deal with a problem? Be seen to do something about it. Mend it. So that problem is solved. The high achiever is congratulated. That is the paradigm that so many of the business theories are based on. Problems are solved and attention is given to the next issue. High achievers are rewarded by focusing on things they can control – systems, performance reviews etc.

How to encourage reflective thinking.

Reflective learning adds a perspective that allows the practitioner to break out of this mould. Reflective learning is a skill that is much more than "mulling something over".

At its simplest it is described as a cycle of inquiry.

When we act on something a change happens, then we reflect on this and that results in actively identifying a change that would mean a different action and so the cycle goes around again. The learner moves from action to reflection and the reflection should result in an action. This turns the everyday practice of reflection into a serious practise of learning.

Action

Reflection

Judi Marshall[3] offers a useful perspective by identifying 2 focuses – she calls them Arcs of Attention that helps us examine what influences are guiding us.

Inner Arcs of Attention what we notice about:	Outer Arcs of Attention what we notice about:
our assumptions our patterns of activity our response to others the language we use the way we make sense of what's going on.	what is going on around us how we are affecting that how we are maintaining or changing a situation how we can test our assumptions how other people are making sense of the same events or situation.

This thoughtful exercise challenges one's assumptions and examines something from another person's point of view. It means understanding the wider field of influence. (Also called Reflexive Thinking.) So for example, going back to our client who moved the goal posts and jeopardised the success of their project: could we have predicted the project might change; was there anything in our proposal that unwittingly pushed them into an action; did we miss the signs; did we talk to the right people when diagnosing? It would be a bold person who did not see how one could do better under this scrutiny.

What makes this distinct from "mulling it over" is the deliberate intent to improve, the discipline of regularly reflecting and, in our practice, we give it a structure and encourage people to write the reflections down in our Change Maker Journal. To begin with most people find it challenging, we are not used to examining our assumptions and actions with such rigour. We recognise that some people will feel vulnerable and in 1:1 coaching we are able to offer a safe environment to explore this.

Case Study:

Katy is a female IT specialist, frustrated by what she observed as the unfriendly reaction she got from her fellow managers. She assumed that "they are not used to a competent woman". This exhibition of sexism in the team was a failure by them and they need to change their attitude. Using the discipline of reflecting on her Inner Arcs and Outer Arcs of Attention she came to the understanding that it may not be her gender they were reacting to – she was strongly extrovert in a room full of mostly introverted people. Bouncing into a meeting was, to their senses, loud and aggressive and they were reacting accordingly. With this new realisation and better understanding she better respected her colleagues and she established a better working relationship.

It was perfectly obvious to assign Katy's problems to sexism in the team, it was the most straight forward assumption. Without structured reflection Katy might never have broken though that barrier.

Reflective Learning in Organisations.

To flourish in today's competitive environment, organisations need their employees to be agile and effective – that isn't about working harder. They need to be thinking creatively about the needs of the organisation. They need to take responsibility for their own behaviour, share information and help and support others to do the same. As Argyris[4] so eloquently puts it "Leaders and subordinates alike – those who ask and those who answer –

must all begin struggling with a new level of self-awareness, candour and responsibility" in order to be able to shape long lasting solutions to fundamental problems.

One of the reasons that reflective learning has only recently gained interest from organisational development specialists is that it examines the uncertain, there is little factual information: what was my instinct; what were my motives/reasons behind the way I behaved; how was my feeling reflected in my actions? Rational behaviour is greatly prized in institutions but this can encourage defensiveness, rationalisation and falling back on familiar solutions. These less helpful behaviours are all recognised in well accepted neuroscience theory as deep wired into our unconscious. We have a tendency to favour certain types of action or behaviour – these are often learnt responses to something that happened some time ago and now it is hard to see similar situations as unique events that require unique solutions. Nevertheless, we still tend to play down the role our feelings and emotions have in determining our actions. Reflective learning recognises the role of these unconscious influences and helps us become conscious of them.

Reflectivity provides real benefits in improving problem solving capacity. Learning from direct experience (action) is more effective with reflective learning – reflective learning makes experience more productive. The learner gains greater ability to evaluate their capability to plan and execute courses of actions to attain goals (self-efficacy) which in turn translates into greater learning.

If reflective learning is so powerful what can organisations do to encourage this practise? In most organisations certainty is prized, when reviews are undertaken the facts take centre stage and motives remain unexamined. Some organisations have taken some steps to allow openness in their culture – this is usually called a 'no-blame' culture. But no-blame is not reflective and actually is anti-reflective. No blame usually results in disagreement being avoided, face-saving and consensus being sought. I also posit most managers are uncomfortable with people taking time to think. Staring out the window or walking the grounds in reflection is not 'doing'.

The reflective habit means everyone develops active responsibility for their own behaviour, owns their accountability – is willing to be vulnerable. Reflecting undefensively allows others to be open too and gives them permission to talk about their role in how things evolved. In a reflexive culture there is less defensive behaviour, more openness and a safe environment to express views. It is a key element in a learning organisation and in rewarding agile practices.

With less defensive behaviour organisations can shape solutions so that they create real change. Employees take an active role in drawing the truth of their own behaviour and motives rather than describing the faults of others. Once people are experienced in being reflective their curiosity will more likely identify problems before they set in, it will be safe for all employees to express concern early. Individuals are more receptive to situations that create problems, they are more agile, they can test their assumptions – after all, like Katy in the example above, we don't know if they are right until they are voiced.

Change management becomes a process of continuous improvement and not the expensive lurching from problem to problem.

Creating a Reflective (Reflexive) Culture.

As a learning methodology reflective learning is incredibly versatile. It crosses all learning styles, visual, auditory, kinaesthetic, as people can choose the best way to address their reflective practise for them. It can be included in all development opportunities.

We encourage the habit by starting our learners with a Change Maker Development Journal - a structured approach to reflective learning. It makes learning an active process – not something that is done to you but, in the practice of reflection, something you do to yourself and take active responsibility in.

It integrates theory and practice. When we introduce new concepts or new ways to interpret ideas the reflective journal guides the user to evaluate how their experiences work for them - can the theories be adapted or modified to be more helpful for that situation? How are they influencing the success or detriment of that problem-solving activity?

It clarifies the learning outcomes of that experience, and what might be included in a plan for next time identifying what would be done differently, with new understandings or values and unexpected things they will have learnt about themself.

For the reflective habit to be most powerful individuals are not only personally reflective but they encourage reflectivity in others. That means creating a safe environment to explore one's doubts and concerns. Coaches know that self-disclosure can help others disclose and grow. We help organisations to create this with innovative co-coaching - self-managed coaching pairs where each challenges the other to stretch their reflective learning. This builds reflection into the culture of the organisation.

With the Change Makers Development Journal and Co-coaching initiatives, the learnt discipline of reflective learning means we can leave a legacy of change makers in organisations long after we have moved on.

"By three methods we may learn wisdom: First, by reflection, which is noblest; Second, by imitation, which is easiest; and third, by experience, which is the bitterest."

Confucius

[1] Making Experience Count: The Role of Reflection in Individual Learning. Di Stefano G, Francesca G, Pisano G & Staats B, Harvard Business School working paper 14-093

[2] Teaching Smart People How to Learn. Argyris C, Harvard Business Review May 1991.

[3] Self-Reflective Inquiry Practices. Marshall, J. (2001)

[4] Good Communication That Blocks Learning. Argyris C, Harvard Business Review July 1994

Nicky Carew has over 30 years' experience of working with senior executives to develop their skills to manage in an increasingly complex environment and has a Masters in Executive Coaching. She lives on the site of 1066 Battle of Hastings and still gets excited by rainbows, watching the International Space Station go overhead and meteor showers.

Contact the Authors

We would love to hear from you. We are keen to share knowledge and thinking with change makers everywhere. We all have so much to learn.

Contact The Change Maker Group via our website www.thechangemakergroup.com or email us at community@thechangemakergroup.com. You will also find us on LinkedIn, Twitter and Facebook. We post regular blogs, articles, videos and snippets – it would be great to get your feedback.

Of course, if you would like to email one of the authors feel free to contact them direct.

Angie Beeston	angie@thechangemakergroup.com
Michelle Brailsford	michelle@thechangemakergroup.com
Nicky Carew	nicky@thechangemakergroup.com
Karen Dempster	karen@thechangemakergroup.com
Julia Felton	julia@thechangemakergroup.com
Richard Flewitt	richard@thechangemakergroup.com
Malcolm Follos	malcolm@thechangemakergroup.com
John Hackett	john@thechangemakergroup.com
Vanda North	vanda@thechangemakergroup.com
Simon Phillips	simon@thechangemakergroup.com
Cathy Summers	cathy@thechangemakergroup.com
David Walker	davidwalker@thechangemakergroup.com

community@thechangemakergroup.com

Printed in Great Britain
by Amazon